RONSARD

POET OF NATURE

RONSARD

POET OF NATURE

by

D. B. WILSON

MANCHESTER
UNIVERSITY PRESS

Preface

RONSARD'S nature poetry has been treated by various critics in articles and has furnished chapters of books,[1] but the treatment has been mainly by anthology and eulogy.[2] There has been no satisfactory account of the way in which Ronsard describes nature, still less of his general idea of nature. In the wider field of French Renaissance poetry as a whole, a small number of articles have appeared,[3] stressing the description of birds, trees, flowers and so on, but ignoring more complicated attitudes towards less obvious meanings of nature.[4] The present essay, which clearly owes a great deal to the investigations of other critics and especially to the brilliant work of M. Marcel Raymond and M. Albert-Marie Schmidt, is intended to fill this gap. Incomplete as it is, it attempts to examine the whole tension between Ronsard and

[1] Cf. H. Guy: *P. de Ronsard, peintre et interprète de la nature* (Grenoble, 1927); P. Laumonier: *Ronsard et sa province* (Paris, n.d.) (an anthology with an introduction); A. Tilley: *Ronsard's poetic growth* (*Mod. Lang. Rev.*, 1934-6). Also chapters in: Laumonier: *Ronsard, poète lyrique* (Paris, 1909); M. Raymond: *L'influence de Ronsard* (Paris, 1927). More recently there has appeared the short general study in G. Gadoffre's *Ronsard par lui-même* (Paris, 1960) which is perhaps the most stimulating of recent contributions in this field.

[2] Cf. especially J. Vianey: *Les grands poètes de la nature en France: Ronsard —La Fontaine* (*Rev. de Cours et Conf.*, 1925).

[3] Cf. especially N. H. Clement: *Nature and the country in 16th and 17th century French poetry* (*PMLA*, 1929); J. Voigt: *Das Naturgefühl in der französischen Renaissance* (Berlin, 1898).

[4] But cf. H. Busson: *Sur la philosophie de Ronsard* (*Rev. de Cours et Conf.*, 1929-30).

the idea of nature and in this way to suggest an approach to what is perhaps the most significant and illuminating aspect of his lyricism.

It is perhaps a happy coincidence that the main meanings which Ronsard attaches to *nature* should follow on from one another as the poet develops, thus enabling our study to be largely chronological. The second chapter deals at length with the traditional type of nature poetry produced by Ronsard and with the differences between his approach to *natura naturata* (the details of Nature's creation) and his descriptive technique, and those of various predecessors. The third chapter deals with *natura naturans* (Nature as a controlling and organizing force)—again a commonplace, although it appears to spring less readily to the critic's mind—and attempts to link Ronsard's description of the greater aspects of the universe with his views on poetry and aesthetics. The fourth chapter, although the shortest, is the keystone to the argument in that it illustrates the way in which, when nearing the end of his poetic career, Ronsard moves towards a point of view in which poetry is clearly associated with temperament[1] and nature with life.

An Appendix has been added in which a number (unfortunately, but necessarily, a very small number) of Ronsard's nature poems have been set down for the convenience of the reader. Here an attempt has been made to include poems not too easily accessible in anthologies. Longer poems have had to be kept out for obvious reasons and the result is intended to supplement and illustrate the essay rather than to present a truly representative canvas of Ronsard's nature poetry.

The actual writing and publication of this book have been

---

[1] The third meaning of nature being, in the words of L. Lemnius' popular reatise, translated into French as: *Les occultes merveilles & secretz de nature* Paris, 1574): 'L'instinct & inclination d'un chascun.'

possible only with the help of many colleagues and friends. I am particularly grateful for the help of M. Raymond Lebègue in Paris, of Professor Mansell Jones and Professor Vinaver in Manchester, and in Durham a number of people including Professor Lough, Dr. Doyle and Dr. Mossop. I have to acknowledge the financial assistance given by the Durham Colleges Research Fund.

Contents

CHAPTER I

The Meanings of 'Nature'

NATURE poetry is seldom concerned merely with the description of the separate phenomena of creation. To mention these things is inevitably to imply a power behind them, to describe them is to introduce the reader to the describer.

In the sixteenth century, the universe is seen very much as a created whole, subject to certain over-riding laws, which govern in the same way all creatures and all phenomena. There is no opposition between Nature and Man such as exists in the work of so many nineteenth-century writers. On the contrary, man is the microcosm of Nature, the *petit univers*,[1] for the universe is continually creating diminutives of itself, whether by the hand of God, or through the

---

[1] Cf. among other examples Cohen, vol. I, p. 324 (Appendix, p. 156), and also A. Chastel: *L'Œuf de Ronsard* (*Mélanges Henri Chamard*, Paris, 1951, pp. 108–11). In the writings of the *Pléiade*, there is an interesting and highly developed passage on the relationship between microcosm and macrocosm in Tyard's *Second Curieux* (ed. J. C. Lapp, New York, 1950, pp. 130 ff.). Ronsard's references are much less specific, e.g.:

> Chef, petit univers, qui montres par effet
> Que tu as du grand Tout parfaite cognoissance.
>
> (Cohen, vol. I, p. 227)

Ronsard's works are quoted throughout this essay and the appendix from the edition by P. Laumonier (*Société des textes français modernes*, Paris, 1914— cont.) whenever possible: otherwise from that by G. Cohen (Gallimard, Paris, 1938). The first of these is abbreviated as Laum., the second as Cohen.

imagination of man. Similarly the writer is the microcosm of the Creator and poetry in particular is above all an imitation, a reflection of the details and variety of Nature. In his first published preface, Ronsard states categorically:

> nulle Poësie se doit louer pour acomplie, si elle ne ressemble la nature, laquelle ne fut estimée belle des anciens, que pour estre inconstante, & variable en ses perfections.[1]

Thus the variety of a Nature that is above all ingenious and artistic[2] calls forth a similar variety from the poet, whose methods of creation are described by Ronsard as being those of the bee, sipping honey from a variety of flowers:

> Mon Passerat, je resemble à l'abeille
> Qui va cueillant tantost la fleur vermeille,
> Tantost la jaune, errant de pré en pré. . . .[3]

This simple, idyllic picture can be contrasted with another: on one occasion at least, the poet emphasizes the duty of imitating nature didactically, as a prophet and under a sort of compulsion:

> La Muse . . . nous blesse & nous rend fantastiques,
> Chagrins, capricieux, hagards, melancholiques,
> Vaisseaux dont Dieu se sert, soit pour profetiser,
> Ou soit pour enseigner . . .
> Les arrests de Nature, & les choses fatales.[4]

---

[1] Laum., vol. I, p. 47. Cf. also the injunctions in the preface to the *Franciade* published in 1587 (Laum., vol. XVI, pp. 334, 345). Also Laum., vol. I, pp. 32, 146, 260; vol. II, pp. 3, 96, etc. . . .

[2] Cf. Laum., vol. VII, p. 230. Nature is also referred to as creating her objects 'd'un art si curieux' (Laum., vol. IX, p. 22) and there are many similar references.

[3] Cohen, vol. II, p. 390. Cf. also Laum., vol. III, p. 23; vol. VII, p. 229; vol. XI, p. 161.

[4] Laum., vol. XVI, p. 355.

However, all this is part of the greater picture:

> Du grand monde la peinture,
> Les chemins de la nature,
> Ou la musique des cieus.[1]

Nature is also a controlling force holding together the sublunar universe, and having links and reverberations within the extralunar universe. Yet, although Ronsard refers to her occasionally as *l'âme du monde*, he does not insist on her autonomy and he imparts to his readers no vision of the magical, alchemical qualities with which Nature had been invested by earlier Italian philosophers. Nature is assumed always to be under the control of God[2] and, although the idea of a vital force behind creation is continually in the background of Ronsard's poetry, which is without doubt one of movement and *maturation*,[3] there is no suggestion that Nature herself is this *spiritus* which appears so plainly in certain passages of his work, especially in *Le Chat* of 1569[4] and the fourth book of the *Franciade* of 1572.[5] God Himself in fact is truly the Creator, although He is to be found with Nature as His associate.[6]

[1] Laum., vol. I, p. 69.

[2] Cf. Le Caron: *Dialogues* (Paris, 1556), f. 91: '...il ne faut recongnoistre autre ame de l'Univers que Dieu...' Also the commonplace recorded, among many other examples, in B. Aneau's emblem book, *Imagination poétique* (Lyons, 1552), p. 11:

> Qui tout en tout est, et en chacun lieu.
> Ame du monde universel, c'est Dieu.

[3] Cf. M. Raymond's article: *Classique et Baroque chez Ronsard* in *Concinnitas* (Bâle, 1944), p. 140: 'Le poète peint la maturation, la poussée secrète des choses, il "peint le passage"...ce que fut, en Ronsard, le sentiment quotidien de l'existence; l'univers lui paraît en perpétuelle métamorphose,...'

[4] Laum., vol. XV, p. 39.   [5] Laum., vol. XVI, pp. 285 ff.

[6] Cf. Laum., vol. VIII, p. 209. Also vol. IV, p. 10; vol. VIII, pp. 148, 154; vol. XII, p. 44; vol. XIV, p. 178, etc. . . .

The precautionary insistence on the omnipotence of a single God is of course a commonplace which goes back at least to Jean de Meung whose

In the whole of Ronsard's poetry we find only one portrait
of Nature, the allegorical figure. It is brief but telling:

> Bien loing derriere toy, mais bien loing par derriere,
> La Nature te suit, Nature bonne mere,
> D'un baston appuyée, à qui mesmes les Dieux
> Font honneur du genoil quand elle vient aux Cieux.[1]

Yet Nature is frequently personified. She is part of the forces
of creation, and her role is only to be disentangled with
difficulty from that of other figures, who at times have similar
parts to play. Thus Peace, Destiny, Fortune all seem to
waver on the frontiers of the part played and the tasks
carried out by Nature herself according to the medieval
tradition.[2] Even Bacchus is referred to as 'Alme Dieu' and
seems from time to time to take over Nature's duties as
controller and balancer of the universe.[3]

Nature is not as narrowly defined and portrayed by Ronsard as she is in the commonplace distichs of other writers of
the century.[4] Even so, she is rigid in her laws, although the

---

Nature is the *chambriere* of God and the universe. It is to be found throughout sixteenth-century writing. Cf. J. Du Monin: *Nouvelles Œuvres* (Paris,
n.d.—1581), L. Le Caron: *Dialogues*, ff. 83 ff. and, a particularly striking
example, P. Paschal, in a letter translated by H. Busson, in his *Rationalisme
de la Renaissance* (Paris, 1922), p. 255: 'Nature...une force sans raison...qui
dépend de Dieu et non de soi. Pythagore...a professé que Dieu est répandu
dans toutes les parties de l'univers, qu'il va et vient sans la nature et communique la vie à tous les êtres vivants... Cela est presque en accord avec notre
religion.'

[1] Laum., vol. VIII, p. 250 (from the *Hymne de l'Eternité*).
[2] Cf. Laum., vol. III, p. 24; vol. IV, p. 45; vol. V, p. 214, etc.
[3] Cf. Laum., vol. V, p. 74; vol. VI, p. 190.
[4] Despite his delight in occasionally confused allegorizing, Ronsard avoids
in general the crude dichotomy of: *Mère: Marâtre* so often used to char-
acterize Nature in the sixteenth century (perhaps the most graphic illustration
of this is to be found in G. de la Perrière's *Morosophie* (Lyons, 1553), p. 42).
We have found only one example of this (Laum., vol. X, p. 75) and the poet
also applies these adjectives once to Promise (Laum., vol. XIII, p. 6). Cf. also
Laum., vol. V, p. 196.

chief of these is a law against rigidity: it is in fact the law of change and temporal mutation: 'Rien sous le ciel ferme ne dure.' [1] This state of inconstancy is held in balance by Nature's own order and, paradoxically, change leads to a fixed rhythm of existence and to a kind of stability. [2]

The working of these laws implies mystery and Nature is in fact full of secrets, in the main deliberately concealed by her, perhaps to provide a challenge to the discoverer. [3] It is part of the poet's task to: 'sçavoir la nature eplucher', [4] and he may do this as a scientist (in the manner of the Peletier du Mans of the *Amour des Amours* [5] or of many another writer of largely mechanical meteorologies), as a poet (usually an orphic poet, as for instance Ronsard himself in his Hymns) or as a contemplator and mystic who sees into the secrets of the universe by the contemplation of creation and especially the heavens.

A further main meaning which Ronsard, in common with other Renaissance writers, gives to the word *nature* is essence or, more simply, make-up. [6] Mankind in general has its nature and, indeed, we may go further and discover that each particular man has his own nature. The source of this nature is not made clear by Ronsard. It is not definitely astrological, as might have been expected; it does not appear to have been infused by God into man, nor is it precisely an equivalent of personality. It depends partly upon one's star: Ronsard himself

[1] Laum., vol. V, p. 166. Cf. also Laum., vol. II, p. 64; vol. VI, p. 117; vol. VIII, p. 225, etc. . . .

[2] Cf. Laum., vol. VIII, p. 68.

[3] Cf. Laum. vol. II, p. 116; vol. V, p. 254; vol. VI, p. 207; vol. VIII, pp. 90, 246, etc. . . .

[4] Laum., vol. VIII, p. 101.

[5] Cf. my article in *Bibl. d'Hum. et Ren.*, 1954, pp. 298 ff.: *The discovery of Nature in the work of Peletier du Mans*.

[6] Cf. Laum., vol. I, p. 171; vol. II, p. 190; vol. VI, p. 213; vol. VIII, pp. 119, 121, 125, 202, etc. . . .

claims to have been born under Saturn, a normal and useful claim for a Renaissance poet and scholar to make.[1] And
it would appear that there is considerable connection between
nature and temperament. The force, whatever it is, is defined
as follows by Ronsard:

> les naifves et naturelles scintilles de l'ame que des la naissance
> tu as receues.. car tout homme dès le naistre reçoit en l'ame je ne
> sçay quelles fatales impressions, qui le contraignent suivre
> plustost son Destin que sa volonté.[2]

In fact it becomes possible for man to be so constrained by
his nature that he is no longer responsible for his actions.
However, despite the forces of nature and the fallibility of
human kind, man remains responsible for his soul.[3]

The poet himself, and poets as a class, have a very special
type of nature:

> J'ay d'une ardente & brusque fantaisie
> Des la mamelle aymé la poësie,
> Ainsi qu'on voit les hommes volontiers
> Ou par destin suivre divers mestiers,
> Ou par l'instinct de leur propre nature...[4]

Nature is in fact responsible for the *invention* of the poet,[5]
imagination and melancholy going hand in hand even in
1556,[6] although Ronsard is careful to say that study and learn-

---

[1] Cf. Chap. IV of this essay. Cf. also Laum., vol. X, pp. 304 ff.

[2] Laum., vol. XVI, p. 333.

[3] Cf. Laum., vol. II, p. 59, and Cohen, vol. II, p. 51; vol. I, p. 789. The
weakness of the nature of man is particularly stressed in Laum., vol. X,
p. 315.

[4] In Laum., vol. XIV, p. 142. Cf. also Laum., vol. II, p. 157; vol. III,
p. 178; vol. X, pp. 293, 305.

[5] Cf. Laum., vol. XIV, pp. 6, 13, 14.

[6] Laum., vol. VII, p. 280.

ing must be added to her primary gifts, the ideal being: 'un esprit naturel elabouré par longues estudes'.[1]

Here again there is some confusion, for nature in this sense is not entirely a matter fixed at birth by the forces of heredity and astrology. Ronsard sets limits to the influence of the stars, which are unable in many instances to over-ride the free will of man. There is also some confusion between Nature and Destiny. The poet himself was intended by Destiny and indeed by family to become a soldier, but it is Fortune who decides otherwise,[2] and although Ronsard's career is changed by Fortune, his temperament seems to remain the same and, although a poet, he continues to be somewhat bellicose and 'difficult':

> Je suis opiniastre, indiscret, fantastique,
> Farouche, soupçonneux, triste & melancolicque,
> Content & non content, mal propre, & mal courtois:...
> Voylà mon natural, mon Grevin, & je croy
> Que tous ceux de mon art ont tels vices que moy.[3]

One's nature being fixed, at least within certain limits, we arrive at a standpoint (one very familiar to the reader of Montaigne) which is neither astrological nor psychological, but moral. No longer is it merely useless, but it is immoral to struggle against one's nature and such a struggle can only lead to disaster. One must accept calmly nature and the coming of old age, even physical shortcomings in love, and one trusts to

[1] Laum., vol. XVI, p. 338. Here we must refer the reader to the detailed study of the relations between *Nature* and *Art* in Chap. V of R. J. Clements: *Critical Theory and Practice of the Pleiade* (Harvard U.P., 1942), which presents rather a different sense of the word *nature* and one on which Ronsard does not insist.

[2] Laum., vol. X, p. 334. Cf. also Laum., vol. II, p. 190; vol. X, p. 333.

[3] Laum., vol. XIV, p. 195 (from an elegy to J. Grévin first published in 1561). Cf. also vol. XIII, p. 248.

the law of nature to keep away ambition.[1] In fact the bene-volence of Nature, our good guide, points out to us a way of life which, not causing any conflict inside us and preserving us from internal stress, must result in happiness and wisdom and the pursuit of a middle way even in the psychological storms of existence and even if one is a poet.[2]

This type of naturalistic philosophy is understandable enough in an age in which intellectual man tends to worship God with a continual feeling at the back of his mind that the distance between God and man can no longer adequately be represented by a number of rungs on a scholastic ladder. Where God is guiding, omnipotent, but undiscoverable, then it is reasonable that man should leave at times his contempla-tion of the extralunar universe (wherein lies all harmony and wisdom) and concentrate his energies and thoughts on sub-lunar nature, acceptance of which is a part of the condition of humanity and of our world of time.

[1] Cohen, vol. II, p. 639.
[2] Cf. Laum., vol. VII, p. 124; vol. VIII, p. 354; vol. X, p. 303; and Cohen, vol. II, p. 634.

CHAPTER II

The Description of Nature—

natura naturata

THE descriptive tradition in which Ronsard began to write is perhaps best illustrated by the following passage from the *Illustrations de Gaule, et Singularitez de Troye*, a prose work published by Jean Lemaire de Belges in 1512–13. The passage seems to have no other purpose in the text save that of decoration and local colour:

> Car icelle valee de Mesaulon est humble et coye, se baissant doucement entre les deux cruppes des montaignes, lesquelles seslievent hautement dun costé et dautre. Et sont richement revestues de pins, sapins, cedres, cypres, ifz, buissetz, et houx, genevre, galles, therebintes, et coques: qui portent la graine descarlate, et de maints autres petis arbustes aromatiques. Et au fons de la valee le plaisant fleuve nommé Xanthus ou Scamander, couloit ses undes aval qui sont verdes et bleues par la reverberation du ciel et des terres prochaines, et bruit taciturnement entre ses rives, lesquelles sont bien peuplées de cannes, roseaux, joncz fluviaux, et autres herbes aquatiques. Entre lesquelz nidifient cygnes, plongeons, plouviers, malars, cercelles, fulliques, louchiers, poulles deaue, et autres oyseaux de riviere. Et dessus les hauts arbres disposez au long du rivage, cestasavoir chesnes, saulx, fresnes, tilleux, allemarches, ormes, plaines, fouteaux, poupliers, myrtes, et lauriers, habitent maintes nouvelles especes doiseaux: dont les plumettes peintes de diverses couleurs sont esparses par dessus lherbe poingnante: si comme phaisans,

herons, pelicans, poulles d'Inde, becasses, grues, butors, cicongnes, corbeaux, cormorans, chauvettes, tortorelles et coulons ramiers.[1]

Wishing to describe a scene, the writer divides it up into aspects. Here, Lemaire describes foreground, middle distance and background and each of these is set before the reader naïvely in list form. Once Lemaire has embarked upon a list he becomes lost in it and this mass of detail, which is surely due to book-learning rather than to observation of the natural scene, dominates and obscures the whole. Unity and coherence vanish before a flood of apparently ill-arranged and chaotic phenomena and we must look hard for the musical and rhetorical effect of such passages.

The technique of description by means of a series of lists is fundamental to the late fifteenth and early sixteenth centuries and is undoubtedly the basis of the *blason*, which is the early sixteenth-century descriptive poem *par excellence*. T. Sebillet, in his *Art poétique* published in 1548, defines the genre as a 'Perpétuéle louenge ou continu vitupére de ce qu'on s'est proposé blasonner.' [2] A.-M. Schmidt objects to this definition and, attempting to revalue the genre in the light of twentieth-century taste, substitutes a much more complicated one:

Un blason ? C'est par essence un poème qui vise, non pas à décrire, mais à évoquer parmi les créatures d'un monde esthétique, dont le poète est l'artiste tyrannique, une chose, une couleur, un contour, une notion. Grâce aux artifices complexes d'une ombrageuse subjectivité, avide de s'anéantir elle-même, le blason tend à une objectivité aussi grande que possible. Dédaignant d'user d'une gamme de correspondances et d'analogies, qu'il tient pour arbitraires, il se flatte, pourtant, d'être,

---

[1] *Illustrations*, Book I, Chap. XXVIII (Lemaire: *Œuvres*, ed. J. Stecher, Louvain, 1882–91, vol. I, p. 201).

[2] *Art poétique françoys*, ed. F. Gaiffe (Paris, 1910), p. 169.

à la fois perçu par tous les sens du lecteur. Extérieurement, il
s'accommode de l'allure d'un charme, d'une litanie, d'une
kyrielle, d'une incantation. Harcelant l'objet qu'il veut trans-
poser et manifester dans un univers absolu en lançant contre lui
une suite d'apostrophes savamment variées et volontairement
monotones, il le ligote peu à peu dans les mailles d'un filet d'or...
qui devient son secours métaphysique, sa cage perpétuelle, sa
défense contre le temps.[1]

However, we may well see this definition as containing a part
of the truth only and as being in part a projection of nineteenth-century literary pretentiousness upon what seems at
first to be early sixteenth-century naïveté of technique. We
must accept gratefully the idea of evocation rather than description in these poems, but much of their magic—that of a
musical variation continually leaving and returning to a
theme—is connected with a lack of coherence, a lack of
relationship between beginning, middle and end. The poet
continually attacks his subject, which is the focal point of a
circle of frequently repetitive qualifications.

Also, whereas the Schmidt definition can be fitted in with
the subtle and predominantly neoplatonic *blasons* of Maurice
Scève, it can scarcely be applied to the following *Blason du
jardin*, published in 1539 by G. Corrozet among his *Blasons
domestiques*:

> Jardin plaisant, doulx, delectable,
> Jardin en tous fruictz profitable,
> Jardin semé de toutes fleurs,
> Painctes de diverses couleurs,
> Comme le lis, la Rose franche,
> L'œillet, & l'aubespine blanche,
> La violette humble & petite...[2]

---

[1] *Poètes du XVIe. siècle*, ed. A.-M. Schmidt (Paris, 1955), p. 293.
[2] G. Corrozet: *Blasons domestiques* (facs. ed. by the *Soc. des Bibliophiles
français*, Paris, 1865), p. 7.

Corrozet himself states that this is a humble genre and indeed appeals to a more learned and skilful successor when he suggests in his preface that his readers should consider him to be:

> le painctre qui sur le tableau avec le pinceau mect la premiere couleur, & compasse les traictz & lineatures de son ouvrage... attendantz que quelque scavante muse les enriche.[1]

Perhaps we may follow these descriptions by one more, again in verse, from a collection of poems by Charles de Sainte-Marthe:

> Jadis il fut un lieu en Thessalie,
> Place, estimée a merveilles jolye,
> Cinq milles pas ayant en sa longueur,
> Six mille aussi en patente largeur,
> Champ delectant par plaisante verdure,
> Champ produissant toute bonne pasture,
> Champ, le vray lieu de toute amenité...[2]

This passage is obviously remarkable for the poverty and lack of coherent individuality of the picture it presents and, in particular, for the writer's inability to choose the meaningful adjective.[3] These characteristics surely lead us to the conclusion that the author is unsure of his viewpoint. We are forced to distinguish between the literary and the moral viewpoint. The latter is the natural possession of one writing on any subject on which he chooses to express a preference or bias, the former only appears when there is a coincidence between the subject and the writer—more simply, when the

---

[1] *Blasons domestiques*, p. 2. In this way, Ronsard himself adds to the simpler, more naïve poetry of C. Marot. Cf. Laum., vol. I, p. 83.

[2] *Poesie françoise* (Paris, 1540), p. 197.

[3] In 1566, Ronsard urges the poet to: 'fuir les epithetes naturelz... comme *la riviere coulante, la verde ramée*...' (Laum., vol. XIV, p. 17).

subject (matter and style) fits in (or, more properly, is made to fit in) with the temperament of the writer who, in his description, distinguishes himself and his emotion from other people viewing or imagining a similar scene.

In the case of the Lemaire description of the valley of Mesaulon, the lists of trees and birds merely reflect the fact that Lemaire knows that such trees and birds are said to exist. In the Corrozet *blason* the adjectives reflect an attitude so single-minded as to be over-simple, and this is even more true in the case of the poem by Sainte-Marthe.

We must beware of suggesting that these descriptions are inferior in value to later, apparently more sophisticated, examples. Although Schmidt is carried away somewhat by his own eloquence, the fact remains that this earlier type of description is deliberately designed. It can properly be seen as one of the many ramifications of the medieval ideal of *amplificatio*.[1] We are so used to the description being centralized, that is to say organized around an emotion or even perhaps a trick of light or a trait of so-called character, that it is something of a shock to contemplate the apparently disorganized— the simple list or development, or the *traictz & lineatures* almost without enrichment but with repetition and development in a *linear* direction.[2]

The enrichment which Corrozet seems to contemplate and which Ronsard is to add was certainly organized according to some central motive and the type of description we shall find in Ronsard's work is governed, not by the desire for length, but by the desire for coherent and concise grouping around a symbol or a feeling, by the wish that the poem should

---

[1] Cf. E. Faral: *Les arts poétiques du XIIe. et du XIIIe. siècle* (Paris, 1924), pp. 74 e.s., and E. Curtius: *European literature and the Latin Middle Ages* (London, 1953), pp. 501 e.s. and 490 e.s.

[2] This adjective is used by Curtius, op. cit., p. 492.

follow, not its own head, but a path determined by neoclassical laws of composition or perhaps by the temperament
of the poet, each part of the poem being enriched and
coloured in the same vein. In fact later generations of poets—
and the work of Ronsard in particular—bring more variety
to the medieval conventions of description, and this would
appear to reflect the variety both of the created world which is
described and of the temperament of the writer who is describing it. In general, the poetry of this century is made up of
images rather than statements and consequently it must make
use of images which vibrate in the same emotional key: once
this is achieved, any moral stated by the writer is over-
whelmed and becomes insignificant.

The late fifteenth and early sixteenth centuries, however,
seem anxious to insist upon the moral viewpoint. It is in fact
normal for poetry of this period, in serving both the ends
declared by Horace to be essential, to lay emphasis upon the
didactic rather than the pleasant, the beautiful or the aesthetic-
ally interesting. The type of these descriptions is to be seen in
a thirteenth-century poem by Philippe de Vitry, Bishop of
Meaux, which is called *Les Dicts de Franc Gontier*.[1] The
rustic current, the *gaulois* simplicity emanating from such
poems is expanded and made more realistic in many writings
of the late fifteenth and early sixteenth centuries. These later
poets stress the didactic note. They are often materialistic and
concerned even principally with the agricultural yield and
details of the fertility of the part of the countryside being described.[2] Again, the ease and simple comforts of the rustic life
are flavoured with an approval of careless and easygoing

---

[1] The best modern text of this poem is to be found in *Romania*, 1898,
p. 61.

[2] Cf. a passage from the *Fleurs et Antiquitez des Gaules* (*Anciennes Poésies
françaises*, ed. A. Montaiglon, Paris, 1855–78, vol. VIII, p. 208).

ways, of the golden mean and of freedom in many descriptions which are often not exempt from coarseness.[1]

The description of nature, however, becomes literary in the hands of Lemaire de Belges, the poet, although the didactic element persists. He stresses particularly the theme of antiquity, already strong in the *Illustrations de Gaule et Singularitez de Troye*,[2] and although he favours the list,[3] in the *Epistres de l'amant vert* more than one passage seems in its rhythmic subtleties and in its plastic life and gaiety to be a forerunner of the nature descriptions published by Ronsard in 1550.[4]

Again, in the poetry of Clément Marot the list type of description is present, but his poetry is closer to that of the *Pléiade* and seems to be conceived in a much more personal fashion. The chief importance of Marot's contribution is in fact the autobiographical note which is sounded in a much less heavy manner than it had been previously.[5] Marot gaily adapts *Franc Gontier* to the requirements of a pseudo-auto-biography[6] and continues this note in two important and well-known passages, one from the *Eglogue au Roy*[7] and one from *L'Enfer*.[8]

A further predecessor of Ronsard in the field of nature poetry is Bonaventure Des Périers, who claims specifically to

[1] Cf. Montaiglon, vol. I, p. 311.

[2] Cf. Book I, Chap. XVI (Stecher, vol. II, p. 152), where a long passage is included 'pource quil est beau et delectable, et sent bien son antiquité'.

[3] Cf. *Concorde des deux langages*, ed. J. Frappier (Paris, 1947), p. 16, and note 66 on p. 61.

[4] Cf. *Les Epîtres de l'amant vert*, ed. Frappier (Geneva, 1948), lines 192–3 and 270 ff. from the first epistle with Ronsard's *De l'election de son sepulcre* (Laum., vol. II, p. 97).

[5] E.g. by J. Froissart: *L'Espinette amoureuse* (*Œuvres—Poésies*, Brussels, 1870, vol. I, pp. 86 ff.).

[6] *Œuvres* (ed. A. Grenier, Paris, n.d.), vol. I, p. 39.

[7] Ibid., pp. 36–7.

[8] Ibid., pp. 54–5.

be following a rustic Muse.[1] His description of the *vendanges* is joyous and highly unclassical, despite the presence of a *satyre* and a nymber of *nymphes*.[2] His poem *De l'Isle*, despite the claim advanced by G. Des Autels that it is the first French ode,[3] is actually a rustic poem in the same tradition and reminds us strongly of Ronsard's more subtle and harmonious *Voyage d'Hercueil*.[4] The poem is too breathless and uncomposed to belong to the more sophisticated neoclassical type of nature description inaugurated by the *Pléiade*. However, it is lively and active and the emphasis is continually on movement: this is the most alive nature poem to be seen before Ronsard and there is gaiety and bustle even among the fishes and the school of Nymphs:

> Les poissons
> Viennent aux sons
> Des rebecs et espinettes,
> Et, loing du fond
> De l'eau, font
> Petites gambadelettes

> Les tant honnestes
> Brunettes
> Nymphes, de Bacchus prochain
> Suivies,
> S'en sont fuyes
> Là hault, pour veoir tout le train;...[5]

In his *Œuvres poétiques* of 1547, J. Peletier du Mans unites a number of the particular qualities and conventions of his predecessors in the field of nature poetry: he does this under

[1] *Œuvres* (ed. L. Lacour, Paris, 1856), vol. I, p. 156.
[2] Ibid., p. 92.
[3] Cf. *Réplique aux furieuses defenses de Louis Meigret* (Lyons, 1551), p. 63.
[4] Laum., vol. III, p. 184. The original title was: *Les Bacchanales*.
[5] Des Périers: *Œuvres*, vol. I, p. 60.

the sign of Horace, and this neoclassical note is especially
apparent in the poem: *Au Sgr Ronsard 'invitant aux champs*.[1]
Here we have the meal in rustic surroundings, the *bon vin* and
the *sentences* typical of the rustic ode according to the recipe
which is to be offered in the *Deffence et Illustration*.[2] Peletier's
description lacks the vitality of Des Périers and even of
Marot and Lemaire, but the picture is well composed and this
lack of liveliness becomes a positive characteristic in a poem
so obviously designed to lead the age into Horatian paths.
There is detailed and charming description of birds, flowers
and *bergerettes*, and one stanza in particular reminds one of the
nature poems to be published by Ronsard in imitation of
Horace and even of Anacreon:

> Nous verrons le ruisseau
> Es prez faisant son tour,
> Avec maint arbrisseau
> Planté tout alentour:
> Mais tant soit clair et soef,
> Si n'en bevrons nous point,
> De bon vin mieux appoint
> Estancherons la soif.[3]

All this poetry written by predecessors of Ronsard, and
particularly the verses of these latter poets—Lemaire, Marot,
Des Périers and Peletier—illustrates the development of a
tradition and a breaking-away from the description rooted in
the idea of digression or amplification. Between the years
1530 and 1550 we see the development of themes, the
popularization of certain components of landscape and the
formation of a vocabulary for nature description in verse.

---

[1] Peletier: *Œuvres poétiques* (ed. L. Séché, Paris, 1904), p. 96.
[2] Ed. H. Chamard (Paris, 1948), p. 113.
[3] *Œuvres poétiques*, ed. cit., p. 98.

We shall now see the extent to which Ronsard's 1550 odes partake of the list description, of the mingling of pleasant and didactic and at the same time of the realistic, the light-hearted and the rustic, of the autobiographical, of a joyousness continually in movement and of a spirit which is consciously Horatian and follows the free and leisurely path of the golden mean.

In 1550, Ronsard published his first important collection of poems, the *Quatre premiers livres des odes*, and the descriptions of nature which we have in these odes follow fairly closely the example set by Peletier du Mans in 1547, when indeed, in all probability, Ronsard was already composing these poems. Leaving aside, as we shall do in general in this study, the question of sources, we find in these odes at least three main natural themes: the straightforward description of a part of the *Vendômois*, certain passages stressing the connection in the poet's mind between the country and his Muse, and finally two poems devoted to the seasons.

It is no part of our task to provide a guide-book to the countryside in the midst of which Ronsard was born.[1] Stripped of the verbiage of praise and blame, the *Vendômois* is a gentle and fertile country. Ronsard himself was born in the *Château de la Possonnière*, a quarter of a mile from the village of Couture. On the slope where the *Château* stands there are still remnants of the forest of *Gâtine* and in the valley near Couture the river Loir winds slowly through the fields, to be joined by its smaller, but faster-running tributary, the Braye. It is a country of woods—in the midst of what remains of the forest of *Gâtine* the mysterious *Etang de Gâtine* can still be found—of undulating fields, many of which bear vines, of

[1] For descriptions of this, see P. Laumonier: *Ronsard et sa province* (Paris, 1909); F. Desonay: *Ronsard, poète de l'amour*, vol. I (Brussels, 1952).

limestone hills, sometimes startlingly abrupt as at Trôo and
Poncé, in which are found natural and artificial caves and
grottoes.

Most of Ronsard's nature poetry of 1550 evokes and describes in some detail this region or a similar one—for it is
difficult to be precise about a countryside so gentle, so
harmonious, so lovely and so unindividual—one which,
furthermore, is so similar in general effect to the landscape
described by Horace and Virgil.

Two poems among these odes are addressed to the *Fontaine
Bellerie*. This stream is commonly held still to exist in a muti-
lated form on the farm near Couture now known locally as the
Belle Iris.[1] Yet the first of Ronsard's descriptions of this
fountain is, with the exception of a banal third verse, an imitation of Horace's ode, *O fons Bandusiae*.[2] However, no
imitation can be exact and a close comparison of the two texts
indicates that Ronsard's is less measured, clumsier and yet
more vital and eccentric than that of Horace—the French
poet is more careful to stress the qualities of life and movement: his stream is noisier and more rustic.

The second poem written to this fountain by Ronsard is
conventional enough[3] but again includes certain brilliant descriptions of detail. Even so, comparatively little of the poem
is directly concerned with the *Fontaine Bellerie*, and this is
perhaps an introduction to the fact that Ronsard, the *poète de la
nature*, celebrated by Guy, Chamard, Jusserand and others, has
in fact left us, among a mass of poetry, relatively few lines concerned with 'nature'; in this part of our study, we shall be con-
sidering, not whole poems, but short passages of description,

[1] Cf. Laum., vol. I, p. 203, note 2.
[2] Horace, Book III, Ode 13.
[3] Laum., vol. II, p. 14 (Appendix, p. 132). Need it be stressed that, at the
time Ronsard wrote this ode, this type of convention was relatively novel?

which are best characterized as *vignettes*. In the poem we are dealing with, the following lines out of a total of twenty directly concern the fountain:

> Argentine fonteine vive
> De qui le beau cristal courant,
> D'une fuite lente, & tardive
> Ressuscite le pré mourant...

The rest of the poem evokes Ceres and the harvest, a number of pastoral rustics and the *bal des Nymphes*. Yet the lines above, simple as they are, illustrate a number of the characteristics of this early descriptive poetry. We are conscious of an insistence upon detail, of an exact but by no means pedantic choice of a small number of epithets, and a desire to be concise in what is perhaps, by implication, not the most important part of this *ode légère*. These characteristics are in obvious contrast to those of descriptions in the early part of the century and appear to represent an almost deliberate reaction against the conscious diffuseness of the medieval description-cum-narrative.[1] The linear type of development is deserted for the poem grouped around one aspect or symbol and, in the nature poems of this collection, Ronsard evidently sees the Loir in particular as the centre, real and symbolic, of the countryside which helped to shape his first poems. Of the 1550 odes, two are addressed to this river. In the first of these it is described simply as:

> Loir, dont le cours heureus distille
> Au sein d'un païs si fertile...
> ... ta parlante rive...[2]

---

[1] It must be emphasized that the opposition observed here is not the medieval one between amplification and abbreviation.

[2] Laum., vol. II, p. 104.

The second is more specific:

> Source d'argent toute pleine,
> Dont le beau cours éternel
> Fuit pour enrichir la plaine
> De mon païs paternel...
>
> Fui donques, heureuse source,
> Et par Vendôme passant,
> Retien la bride à ta cource
> Le beau cristal effaçant.
>
> Puis saluë mon la Haie
> Du murmure de tes flots,...
>
> Va donc, & reçoi ces roses
> Que je repan au giron
> De toi source qui aroses
> Mon païs à l'environ,...
>
> Ne noiant ses pastourages
> D'eau par trop se repandant,
> Ne deffraudant les ouvrages
> Du laboureur atandant,
>
> Mais favorable & utile
> Lui riant joieusement,
> Fai que ton onde distile
> Par ses champs heureusement:...[1]

In both these descriptions, we see characteristics similar to those already noted in the poems addressed to the *Fontaine Bellerie*. Here there is more detail, particularly of sound,[2] and

[1] Ibid., p. 129.

[2] Ronsard is always chiefly concerned with the senses of sight and hearing, acknowledged to be the respectable literary senses by the Renaissance, and especially by the fifteenth- and sixteenth-century neoplatonists.

we are conscious of a proud note of regional patriotism, together with an impression of utility and fertility, and joy in movement allied to the idea of growth. Similar themes recur in Ronsard's descriptions of the *Vendômois* itself.

In general, Ronsard is inclined to seek out the particular corner and describe the small but significant detail in a *vignette*. In the first of his poems to the *Vendômois*, however, there is an exact pictorial presentation of the region.

> Deus longs tertres t'emmurent,
> Dont les flancs durs & fors
> Des fiers vents qui murmurent
> S'opposent aus effors.
>
> Sur l'un Gâtine sainte
> Mere des demidieus,
> Sa teste de verd painte,
> Envoie jusque aus cieus,
>
> Et sur l'autre prend vie
> Maint beau sep, dont le vin
> Porte bien peu d'envie
> Au vignoble Angevin.[1]

The Loir itself is described again in two stanzas, but the description tends towards the general, and no new *motif* is introduced. Precision and conciseness are wooed with success, although the epithet *tard à la fuite* is one which appears often enough in Ronsard's poetry and it begins to be *homeric* and almost *naturel*.[2] Even so, it is neat and telling in itself.

A second *Vendômois* river, the Braye, whose waters move 'fortement' in contrast to those of the Loir, 'plus lentement', [3]

---

[1] Laum., vol. I, p. 222 (Appendix, p. 129).

[2] For this sense of the word *naturel*, cf. Laum., vol. XIV, p. 17.

[3] Laum., vol. II, p. 92.

brings a note of variety in a simple enough form to a further poem dedicated to the region. In all these poems the utilitarian, if sparkling picture of steady, happy fertility is disturbed by the introduction of Muses, Graces, Nymphs and a certain holy forest, the *Forêt de Gâtine*, which is the subject of a further poem. Written deliberately and artificially 'on a high level', however, these lines suggest that the young Ronsard was not yet fully in control of the conventional and the mythological. Despite the praises of a contemporary critic,[1] the following lines, for example, are little more than a literary exercise:

> Courbant'en bas les cheveus vers
> De ta sime ploiante...[2]

and a number of ugly lines disfigure the poem:

> M'aléges & defasches...
> ... l'oreille oiante...

We may add to these poems specifically addressed to the countryside where Ronsard spent his youth two stanzas from the ode, *De l'election de son sepulcre*. In general the landscape of this ode does not seem in tune with the picture we have already seen of the *Vendômois* as a happy, smiling, fertile region. Here we have the 'roches hautaines' and other features of the conventional petrarchist landscape, including the apostrophizing typical of such poetry. The poem moves jerkily (but understandably—its structure is simple to analyse) from one *classical* episode to another. Yet, despite the rather awkward handling of an imperfectly assimilated mythology by episodes and aspects, two stanzas, later omitted by the poet, perhaps because he recognized them to be out of key with the rest, must be mentioned here, as they describe

---

[1] Cf. A. Fouquelin: *Rhétorique françoise* (Paris, 1555), p. 19.
[2] Laum., vol. I, p. 245.

in detail the *île verte* (as it is still known) which stood at the
confluence of the Loir and the Braye:

> ... en cette isle verte
> Où la course entrouverte
> Du Loir, autour coulant,
> Est accolant'.

> Là où Braie s'amie
> D'une eau non endormie,
> Murmure à l'environ
> De son giron.[1]

To sum up what we have observed in this, Ronsard's first
published collection of poems, it is evident that natural
phenomena are treated symbolically: water, for example,
signifies for the poet movement, sparkle, change. It is a
feature which runs through the local landscape, just as these
three characteristics run through the poetry of Ronsard at this
time, and we must accept the fact that movement, sparkle and
change are more important to Ronsard than water and the
pictorial qualities of the landscape which he is trying to convey. These three qualities illustrate a mood, they betray a
constant need in the poet's mind for variety and *inconstance*,[2]
and an associated need to convey this variety in terms of the
image.

Indeed, the poems scarcely put before us individual masses
of water. They make use indifferently of certain catch-phrases:
beau cristal, cours, courant, heureus, distille, fertile and so on.
In fact the passage describing the *Fontaine Bellerie*[3] needs only
minor changes or slight inattention on the reader's part to
make it applicable to the Loir, and the Loir itself is distin-

[1] Laum., vol. II, p. 98.
[2] Cf. the preface to the *Quatre premiers livres des odes* (Laum., vol. I, p. 47).
[3] Laum., vol. II, p. 14.

guished from the Braye merely by a rather commonplace antithesis, almost as neat, almost as poverty-stricken as the Horatian distinction between the Liris and the Anio.[1] Yet there are passages which give us a foretaste of a more mature artist, and when Ronsard compares his poetry and that of Du Bellay with:

> ce lieu... où le grand fleuve de Loire
> Se mesle avec un plus grand Dieu[2]

we catch a glimpse of the sweep of later poems such as the *Ode à Michel de l'Hospital*[3] which do indeed seem to follow the winding of a great river, whose slow stream is nevertheless disturbed here and there by eddies which might be called *baroque*.

A different type of landscape again is seen in *A Caliope*.[4] In this imitation of Horace, Ronsard evokes a desert landscape, where solitude rather than picturesque detail is the aim of the seeker after nature. It is not even suggested that these scenes be associated with the savage and *horror-filled* wildness of the forest of *Gâtine*—in fact the poet is evoking a state of mind, that of the poet, and he does this in a fashion which is almost a commentary on a few lines from the *Deffence et Illustration*:[5]

> Les uns ayment les fresches umbres des forestz, les clers ruisselez doucement murmurans parmy les prez ornez & tapissez de verdure... Bien te veux-je avertir de chercher la solitude & le silence amy des Muses...

---

[1] Horace: *Odes*, Book I, Odes 7 and 31. In this connection we must remember a passage from the *Avertissement* to the 1550 edition of the odes: 'Au surplus, lecteur, tu ne seras émerveillé si je redi souvent mémes mots, mémes sentences, & mémes trais de vers, en cela imitateur des poëtes Grecs, & principalement d'Homere,...' Ronsard's picture of the Loir, moreover, is varied in 1552 by a description of this river in flood (Laum., vol. IV, p. 169).

[2] Laum., vol. II, p. 37.   [3] Laum., vol. III, p. 118.

[4] Laum., vol. I, p. 177.   [5] *Deffence et Illustration*, p. 169.

When Ronsard finds that the *Vendômois* landscape is in-
sufficient to convey the full variety of poetic themes and moods
which inspire him, he invents or imitates other types of
picture, as in *De l'election*, where a Petrarchan landscape is
apostrophized rather in the manner of Lemaire de Belges, or
in *A Caliope*, where we are introduced into a solitude which is
scarcely *Vendômois*. One may even go so far as to say that
there is a lack of personal *nuance* and idiosyncrasy, which
makes for a rather stiff poetical world. Convention is carried
still further in certain poems of 1550 which develop a decorative technique which appears to be mainly italianate. *Des Roses
plantées pres un Blé*[1] can only be described as 'preanacreontic'
in style and contains little true description. The set tableaux
of *Le ravissement de Cephale* and the *Defloration de Lede*[2] contain descriptions which are obviously dissociated from the
observation of the countryside and connected with the plastic
arts. We may perhaps attribute these tableaux to what has been
regarded as a misunderstanding of Horace's phrase: *Ut pictura
poesis*: their main characteristic is a neo-Italian frilliness which
is the reverse of rustic. And, although this type of description
is exceptional in Ronsard's work at this time, for the poet is
genuinely concerned with the consolation he receives from
and the affection he feels for the green landscapes of the
Vendômois,[3] we should perhaps quote two short descriptions

---

[1] Laum., vol. II, p. 124.   [2] Ibid., pp. 133 and 67.

[3] Here we cannot forbear to mention Ficino's *De vita libri tres*, translated
as: *Les trois livres de la vie* (Paris, 1581). We quote from pp. 20, 65, 123 ff.,
although it seems probable that, had Ronsard suspected this identity of tastes
between himself and the Florentine, he would have proclaimed it.

'Nous louons le frequent regard d'une eau claire & nette, la couleur verte,
& rouge, l'usage des jardins, & des forests, le pourmener jouxte le rivage des
fleuves & a travers les prez plaisans & delicieux.... Ce pendant nous pro-
menans entre les bois, boccages, ou prez verdoyans, nous rechercherons la
cause pourquoy la verte couleur sur toutes nourrit, entretient, & delecte la
veüe salubrement,...'

which are not without influence on later poets[1] and which illustrate admirably the static and even stilted beauty to which Ronsard occasionally gives his allegiance at this time:

> La mer est painte plus bas,
> L'eau ride si bien sur elle,
> Qu'un pescheur ne nîroit pas
> Qu'elle ne fust naturelle.
> Ce soleil tumbant au soir
> Dedans l'onde voisine entre,
> A chef bas se laissant cheoir
> Jusqu'au fond de ce grand ventre.
>
> Sur le sourci d'un rocher
> Un pasteur le loup regarde,
> Qui se haste d'aprocher
> Du couard peuple qu'il garde:
> Mais de cela ne lui chaut,
> Tant un limas lui agrée,
> Qui lentement monte en haut
> D'un lis, au bas de la prée.[2]

And again:

> D'assés loin tu vois redoublé
>   Dans le blé
> Ta joue de cinabre teinte,
> Dans le blé qu'on voit rejouir
>   De jouir
> De ton image en son verd peinte.[3]

Two of Ronsard's 1550 odes describe not particular landscapes, but the general aspect of a fertile countryside in

[1] One thinks immediately of Théophile de Viau.
[2] Laum., vol. II, p. 72.
[3] Ibid., p. 125.

particular seasons—Spring and Summer. The description of
Spring is especially interesting because we are able to compare
it on the one hand with a passage by Peletier du Mans (of
which we have two versions), on the other with the source
used by Peletier and by Ronsard, from Virgil's *Georgics*. But
while it fits into the tradition of neoclassical, pseudo-antique
poetry, it also breaks with a tradition, being very different
from the type of evocation to be seen *par excellence* at the
beginning of the *Roman de la Rose*, one which is repeated
many times by the *Rhétoriqueurs*, by Lemaire de Belges and
by Clément Marot, who all perpetuate this picture of an
allegorical and a static Spring, pastoral but unenergetic in the
manner of Guillaume de Lorris. Ronsard abandons this
inspiration and, following Virgil, absorbs into his description
a genuine realization of the movement and the powers of an
inconstant and varied Nature.

Virgil's description is ritual, serious and conscious of the
forces of an anthropomorphic Nature, expressed through a
series of deities who are on the whole dignified. Peletier
translates this text somewhat eccentrically in 1547, and in 1555
this primitive version is further blunted by the poet's efforts
in the direction of regularity of style and rhyme. Ronsard's
text is livelier and, in parts, is even coarsely realistic:

> Ja le ciel d'amour s'enflame,
> Et dans le sein de sa fame...
> Va son ventre ensemanssant...[1]

His description suggests concern with detail rather than with
the whole rhythm of the seasons, and the individual aspects of
Spring are given more relief, even more eccentricity than in

---

[1] The descriptions of Spring which we are concerned with are to be found:
Georgics, Book I, lines 323 ff. Peletier: *Œuvres poétiques* (de 1547), p. 87, and
L'Amour des Amours (pub. 1555), p. 131; Ronsard: Laum., vol. I, p. 150.

Virgil; they move in a less co-ordinated fashion and this movement is important to the poet for its own sake:

> Ja le beau printens arive,
> Et ja l'herbe de la rive
> Sousleve un petit son chef,
> Et méprisant la froidure
> Etalle aus cieus sa verdure
> Pour i fleurir de rechef.

Ronsard rejoices in movement at this time. As he says elsewhere:

> Ma painture n'est pas mue
> Mais vive, & par l'univers
> Guindée en l'air se remue
> De sus l'engin de mes vers.[1]

Even so, his thoughts, as Virgil's, turn from the movement of
a series of personified forces in the Spring to the celebration of
a nostalgic picture of an eternal Spring in the Golden Age.

The poem in this same collection which describes Summer—
De la Venue de l'Esté—is less important to our study, but is an
excellent example of the poet's use of the Virgilian periphrasis.
As he says later on in his career: 'Les excellens Poëtes nomment
peu souvent les choses par leur nom propre'.[2] Yet this poem is
tied down to earth by a certain sprinkling of realistic detail so
that it hovers, as it were, between the world of appearances
and that of imagination:

> Ici, la diligente troupe
> Des ménagers renverse, & coupe
> Le poil de Ceres jaunissant,...
> Ce pendant leurs femmes sont prestes
> D'assurer au haut de leurs testes

---

[1] Laum., vol. II, p. 148.   [2] Laum., vol. XVI, p. 333.

> Des plats de bois, ou des baris...
> Pour aller apâter la peine
> De leurs laborieus maris...[1]

To this picture the book of Odes published by Ronsard in 1552[2] adds certain new elements. Some passages of these odes and other poems published between 1550 and 1552 anticipate a type of nature description to be examined in our second chapter, as they present a number of 'scientific' commonplaces, such as the distinction between the sublunar and the extralunar worlds,[3] and a number of symbolic themes, such as the *bal des estoiles*, the dance of the Muses and the ideal of poetic contemplation in solitude.[4]

The most important poem of this collection—the *Ode à Michel de l'Hospital*—puts before us a strange series of vignettes from nature as a background to a poem which is obviously intended to realize the Ronsardian ideal of the poetic fable which 'teaches' in action. The ode begins peacefully—the idea of gathering a bouquet of flowers is a poetic commonplace of the period[5] although it is presented in an aura of neoclassical magic and mystery—an aura which reappears in the *Antistrophe*:

> Memoyre royne d'Eleuthere,
> Par neuf baisers qu'elle receut
> De Juppiter qui la fist mere,
> En neuf soirs neuf filles conceut.
> Mais quand la Lune vagabonde
> Eut courbé douze fois en rond,...

---

[1] Laum., vol. II, p. 24.
[2] *Le Cinquiesme Livre des Odes*: Laum., vol. III, p. 87.
[3] Cf. ibid., vol. III, pp. 6, 45–6.
[4] Cf. ibid., pp. 100, 150.
[5] Ibid., p. 119.

But this gentle picture of growth:

> Aussi tost que leur petitesse
> Glissante avec les paz du temps,
> Eut d'une rempente vitesse
> Touché la borne de sept ans:...

then receives a sudden push of movement. The bouquet becomes 'un tortis de violettes', the nine daughters leave the quiet pastoral surroundings of their youth and:

> Voyant le front des eaux cruelles
> S'effroyerent d'une grand' peur:
> Et presque cheurent an arriere
> Tant l'horreur les plyoit adonc,
> Comme on voit dans une riviere
> Soubz le vent se courber un jonc:...

However, they then pass the barrier which separates their childhood from their maturity and the beginnings of their power over poets and, through them, over men; and their passage through this barrier is so distinctly *baroque* as to be out of tone with the beginnings of the poem:

> Elles adonc voyant la trace
> De leur Mere, qui ja sondoit
> Le creux du plus humide espace
> Qu'à coups de braz elle fendoit:
> A chef tourné sont devalées
> Penchant bas la teste & les yeulx
> Dans le sein des Pleines salées:
> L'eau qui jaillit jusques aux cieulx
> Grondant sus elles se regorge,
> Et frizant deça & delà
> Mille tortiz, les avala
> Dedans le gouffre de sa gorge.

The description of the palace of Neptune enhances and

enlarges the *baroque* picture built up in the mind of the reader. The tone mounts as the sisters sing their three songs in a crescendo and it remains on a lofty note as they utter their request to Jupiter. Here we come to the main lesson of the poem: an exposition of the doctrine of poetic fury as Ronsard envisages it at this time: not in the manner of the Florentine Academy, but rather as a climax, a type of poetic orgasm, and not by any means as a step on the road towards an ideal of harmony.[1] Yet the ode itself does arrive at harmony. With a description of the Muses and their departure (much less startling than their arrival), we leave the *daimons*, the *eaux solitaires* for a calm landscape where 'Il n'y a ne torrent, ne roche' and where we are able to savour the memory of the 'chanson' and 'Les repliz de sa façon'.[2]

And elsewhere in the 1552 odes we can linger in a calmer world: the landscape of the garden of the Muses, their crystal fountains[3] and, once again, their dance in the light of the moon. This picture is no less 'real' than the vignettes of the *Hospital* ode, and it presents a nature as closely related to the subject of the poem. Already, it would seem, Ronsard has left the field of description, of the *blason* under another name, for the field of imaginative natural images which accompany and reinforce a poem in the manner of fables. Mere enumeration, even of mythological legends, is sacrificed to a more concise and cogent type of decoration, and the digression favoured by the *Rhétoriqueurs* is reduced in scope and fitted, sometimes clumsily enough,[4] into the body of the poem.

Among the poems published in 1550 were two less

[1] Cf. Laum., vol. I, p. 65. Obviously, however, such descriptions of the poetic malady are not to be taken too literally.

[2] Laum., vol. III, p. 163.

[3] Ibid., p. 167.

[4] Cf. *De l'election de son sepulcre.*

'dignified' and serious than the rest: the *Chant de Folie à Bacchus* and *Contre Denise Sorçiere*.[1]

The second of these is the more important. It is inspired by Horace, but it has been said that there may well be an auto-biographical source, and commentators have suggested that Couture possessed its local witch. Be that as it may, the atmosphere of the poem is very different from that of the descriptions of the *Vendômois* we have so far encountered, and its picture of night, loneliness and horror in the pale light of the moon takes us right away from their gentle mood. It may be connected with the following passage, very similar in atmosphere, from the *Folastries*:

> ... puis ceste bonne
> Bonne putain, vas pas à pas...
> Entre les croix du Cimetiere...
> D'un drap mortuere voilée,
> Tant qu'elle, & la nuit étoilée,
> Ayent fait peur au plus hardi,
> Qui passant là le mécredi
> Vient de la Chartre, ou de la foire
> De l'Avardin, ou de Montoire.[2]

But this is a side of what appears to be the life of the village of Couture which Ronsard does not emphasize elsewhere. The picture is realistic in tone if not in expression and, together with certain passages from the *Chant de Folie*,[3] it transports us immediately into an atmosphere which is that of Ronsard's frankly rustic and *gaulois* poetry—that of the *Folastries* and the *Voyage d'Hercueil*.

The *Voyage d'Herceuil*[4] is a poem written to describe and to celebrate a picnic by Ronsard and the *Brigade*, one of the excursions to the country on the fringe of Paris which were so

[1] Laum., vol. II, p. 177; vol. I, p. 238. [2] Laum., vol. V, p. 24.
[3] Cf. Laum., vol. II, p. 178. [4] Laum., vol. III, pp. 184 ff.

popular among writers of the century. Rabelais mentions a similar outing. Pierre Belon describes one also.[1] In fact this poem is the work of a student having a day's respite and a picnic in the country. It is joyous and light-heartedly pedantic. It depends for its effect mainly on the winding together of a skein of different types of movement: the roll-call of the names of members of the *Brigade*, the picnic with its butterfly hunt and its baptism, the reading of verse form three separate parts, held together by the descriptions of nature which form a living and moving backcloth. The whole atmosphere and tempo of the poem is one of haste rather than dignity, and Ronsard stresses that, for today at least:

> ... moy dont la basse Idée
> N'est guindée
> Dessus un cable si hault,...
> En lieu de telles merveilles,
> Deux bouteilles
> Je pendray sus mes rougnons...

The poem is not lacking in the conventional background of *fury*, but this poetic sacredness is the target for robust and perhaps slightly blasphemous fun.

The *Voyage* goes into action in the first few lines, in which the dawn is personified—its movement vies with the movement and preparations of the *Brigade* for, before the dawn, the picnic party is named and sets out joyously and in happy expectation of a meal in the true *gaulois* tradition; they become drunk, chase butterflies which fly delightfully and in shimmering motion before the party. They undergo baptism, drinks toasts to their lady-loves, and, subsiding, listen in grave silence to Dorat as he reads verse.

[1] F. Rabelais: *Œuvres* (Gallimard, Paris, 1942), p. 99; and cf. H. Chamard: *Histoire de la Pléiade* (Paris, 1939–40), vol. I, p. 127.

All this happens against the background of a landscape perfectly suited to the mood and movement of the rest of the
poem: a background, moreover, which is surprisingly exact in
its description of the *Hercueil* scene.

The variegated nature of this description is shown immediately in the first stanza: the note is struck by the *bigarrement* of
the colouring of dawn; this is contrasted with night and the
moon which: 'La nuict brune / Traisne de ses noirs chevaux'.
This force of night acts as a background to the passage, and its
slow, quiet, dark movement opens and concludes the poem,
putting the central, rapid, *baroque* themes of action between
brackets, as it were.

The picnic takes place in a familiar Ronsardian setting, in
which movement and sound are intermingled. The dawn
brings a change, and more movement:

> Iö comme ces saulayes,
>   Et ces hayes,
> Sentent l'humide fraischeur,
> Et ces herbes, & ces plaines
>   Toutes pleines
> De rousoyante blancheur.
>
> Que ces rives escumeuses
>   Sont fumeuses,
> Au premier trait de Phebus!
> Et ces fontainieres prées,
>   Diaprées
> De mille tapis herbus.

The wine and mysterious poetic ecstasy bring an apparently
imaginary landscape before the poet:

> Je voy cent bestes nouvelles
> Pleines d'ailes
> Sus noz testes revoler...

but these creatures are merely butterflies, and the realistic description of the detail which follows puts us perhaps into the mood for one of the most real and evocative of Ronsard's descriptions of a landscape: the landscape of *Hercueil*:

> Iö je voy la valée,
> Avalée
> Entre deux tertres bossus,
> Et le double arc qui emmure
> Le murmure
> De deux ruyseletz moussus.

Finally we are led down from this rush and this ecstasy in the quiet, gentle reading of Dorat and the slow beauty of the evening unfolding itself and leading us into the concluding lines of the poem:

> Ha Vesper, brunette estoyle,
> Qui d'un voyle
> Par tout embrunis les cieulx,
> Las, en ma faveur encore
> Ne decore
> Ta grand' vouste de ses yeulx:
>
> Tarde un peu noyre courriere
> Ta lumiere...
> Donque, puis que la nuict sombre
> Pleine d'ombre,
> Vient les montaignes saisir,
> Retournon trouppe gentille
> Dans la ville
> Demysoulez de plaisir.

And so to bed with the trite if well-expressed moral in the last stanza of the poem: a touch which emphasizes the fact, already implicit in so much of the piece, that we are not deal-

ing merely with the determinedly trivial, that this is definitely
a poem written by a *studieux*, and that it is a *learned* holiday
poem.

In Ronsard's *Folastries* we do indeed come across passages
of nature description which are very much in the same tone as
those we have considered in his first odes, published in 1550,
three years earlier.[1] Yet there are many less conventional
passages in this collection, including what for the sixteenth
century is an extensive description of Winter[2] which is not
merely in the *gaulois* tradition.[3] The strangest of the landscapes in the *Folastries* is, paradoxically enough, a cloud-
scape and comes from the poem, *Le Nuage, ou L'yvrongne*:

> Je voy deça, je voy dela,
> Je voy mille bestes cornues,
> Mille marmotz dedans les nues:
> De l'une sort un grand Toreau,
> Sur l'autre sautelle un chevreau:
> L'une a les cornes d'un Satyre,
> Et du ventre de l'autre, tire
> Un Cocodrile mille tours.
>
> Je voy des villes, & des tours,
> J'en-voy de rouges, & de vertes,
> Voy-les-là, je les voy couvertes
> De sucres, & de poix confis.
> J'en-voy de mors, j'en voy de vifz,
> J'en-voy, voyez-les donq! qui semblent
> Aux blez qui soubz la bize tremblent.
>
> J'avise un camp de Nains armez.
> J'en-voy qui ne sont point formez,
> Tronçez de cuisses, & de jambes,...[4]

and so on for eighty lines.

---

[1] Cf. Laum., vol. V, p. 30.   [2] Ibid., p. 44.
[3] Cf. ibid., p. 31.   [4] Ibid., p. 48.

This picture of nature is strangely unrelated to the human and certainly has no connection with fertility: it is attached to fantastic and exotic peoples and animals and seems to consist of the making-up of pictures entirely for their own sake—not a very common thing for Ronsard. These pictures are put into rhyme, but do not seem to be otherwise controlled and, although perhaps their very lack of control may be seen as symbolic, they are certainly not part of an ordered and considered universe, and there is no attempt to treat clouds scientifically as a meteorological phenomenon.

This cloud-universe reminds us perhaps of the background of the *Hymne des Daimons* (which makes use of a similar picture[1]) in its acknowledgement and celebration of the presence of uncontrolled and even spontaneous forces in the universe, but it is perhaps only a rather exaggerated extension, and a playful one, of the inspiration due to poetry and to the gifts of Bacchus:

> ... le bon Pere joyeux
> Qui se transforme en cent nouvelles.[2]

*   *   *   *   *

The *Amours*, addressed to Cassandre and published in 1552, contain certain basic conventions. This, as always, begs the question of so-called originality, but it is useful to register, here a borrowing from Petrarch, there one from the stock of the neoplatonists, and so on. Certain assumptions are made by the poet and passed on to the reader. We see a nature that is

[1] Laum., vol. VIII, p. 120.

[2] Laum., vol. V, p. 51. It would seem that clouds had considerable fascination for Ronsard who returns to them again in *Les Nues, ou Nouvelles* in 1565, where the output of his fantasy is much more controlled and is indeed expressed in twenty lines only (Laum., vol. XIII, p. 268). Cf. also vol. VII, p. 278; vol. XI, p. 163.

partly *Vendômois*, but which is particularly rich in solitude, which is preferred for once to the picturesque. Features of the natural world are used as very simple symbols, and it is instructive to compare the features used by Ronsard with those which appear in Petrarch's sonnets. In general Ronsard uses roses and lilies, the colours of flesh and of fleshly youth; Petrarch emphasizes the serene, angelic, sweet and gentle nature of his love, her forehead and her chin, all of which betray the soul behind. Ronsard mentions the hands, the neck and the ear and 'de ce sein les boutons verdeletz': the atmosphere is in fact one of sensual rather than spiritual adoration, although the fleshly aspect of love is much less apparent in 1552 than in the 1553 edition of the *Amours*.[1]

Scientific clichés appear, and love is frequently compared to the natural forces of the sublunar world. In general, the use of antithesis is typical of Renaissance theories of the equilibrium of the universe,[2] and different sonnets speak more or less superficially of the soul of the universe,[3] the atoms of Epicurus,[4] the development of harmony from chaos,[5] the entelechy,[6] the theory that the universe is all developed from water and fire,[7] and the cycle of the Moon compared with that of love.[8]

Neoplatonism contributes directly to some of the sonnets,[9] as does Petrarch's feeling that the universe is dominated and obsessed by his love and the spirit (sometimes translated into physical forms) of his loved one. The reader feels the image of the poet's love as being, in a way, the *soul* which holds

[1] Cf Laum., vol. V, pp. 107, 110, etc.

[2] Laum., vol. IV, passim: there are many examples of this type of thing: love is made up of hot and cold, sad and joyful, and so on. The two best examples of this appear to be Laum., vol. IV, pp. 16 and 139.

[3] Laum., vol. IV, p. 29.   [4] Ibid., p. 40.   [5] Ibid., p. 45.
[6] Ibid., pp. 58–9.   [7] Ibid., p. 70.   [8] Ibid., p. 116.
[9] Ibid., pp. 134–5; 141; 149.

D

together and moves behind a world of frequently conventional symbolism. This love is continually immanent in all nature,[1] and the landscape is animated and transformed by her presence, which is only in part physical.[2] Even in poems in which *Vendômois* place-names predominate, they merely serve to enhance and give a certain fugitive individuality to passages in which what Laumonier calls *l'obsession amoureuse* is paramount:

> Saincte Gastine, heureuse secretaire
> De mes ennuis, qui respons en ton bois,
> Ores en haulte, ores en basse voix,
> Aux longz souspirs que mon cœur ne peult taire:
>   Loyr, qui refrains la course voulontaire
> Du plus courant de tes flotz vandomoys,
> Quand accuser ceste beaulté tu m'ois,
> De qui tousjours je m'affame & m'altere:...[3]

As love dominates the landscape and background of these poems, so we may say that the temperament of the poet (of whom the love and the loved one are merely a projection) over-masters the love, dictating the way in which it is felt and expressed. One may even say that on occasion feelings similar to those of the nineteenth-century Romantic poets transfigure a *Vendômois* landscape in these Petrarchan lines:

> Ici, Bayf, où le mont de Sabut
> Charge de vins son espaulle féconde,
> Pensif je voy la fuite vagabonde
> Du Loyr qui traisne à la mer son tribut.
> Ores un antre, or un desert sauvage,
> Ore me plaist le segret d'un rivage,

---

[1] Laum., vol. IV, p. 32. Cf. also pp. 62, 123. [2] Cf. ibid., pp. 109, 127.
[3] Ibid., p. 128.

Pour essayer de tromper mon ennuy:
Mais quelque horreur de forest qui me tienne,
Faire ne puis qu'Amour tousjours ne vienne,
Parlant à moy, & moy tousjours à luy.[1]

This poetry is determinedly non-realistic, and here in particular Ronsard joins the Petrarchans, the neoplatonists and
perhaps even Scève himself. Here is a poetry of absence, in
which the dream is preferred to the reality and the facts of
imagination to the impressions of present phenomena. And,
as in the work of all neoplatonic poets, the task of imagination
and of art is to push memory into the background.

The psychological as well as the natural background con-
forms to these conventions and we come to believe (whatever
the biographical 'facts' of the matter) that Pasquier is right in
suggesting that 'en ses premieres Amours il voulut contenter
son esprit'.[2] In fact, Ronsard's dreams and soliloquies seem
similar to those of the one-eyed Polyphemus who says in the
pastoral poem published in 1560:

... feindre d'estre ayme...
Allege bien souvent l'amoureux qui se veult
Soymesme se tromper, se garissant la playe
Aussi bien par le faux que par la chose vraye.[3]

The *inconstant* and antithetical nature of the sentiments
registered in this Petrarchan poetry again suggests the
va-et-vient of the Ronsardian universe and temperament, and
to that extent the poems are both intensely personal and
'literary', to use the term applied to them by Laumonier,
Lebègue and other critics.

The 'new style' of the poet, as he himself call, it, begins to
crystallize between the years 1553 and 1556. He speaks

[1] Ibid., p. 129. [2] Cf. Laum., vol. X, p. 291, note.
[3] Ibid., p. 290.

solemnly of the laws of nature, most of which govern a process of continual change. Yet the variety of nature in this
sense is rather schematic. For example, of the two poems
dedicated to Ambroise de la Porte in successive years[1] one
deals with the miseries of mankind and human life, the other,
written from the country, with the joys of rustic life and
rustic sports. Immediately we think of the pair of popular
treatises published by Boaistuau in the same year (1558): the
Ample discours des misères humaines and the *Bref discours de
l'excellence et dignité de l'homme.* Such *tours de force* are
evidently related, in so far as they impinge upon the history of
ideas, to the extremely popular genre of the paradox, in which
any surprising theme was developed, often alongside its
antithesis.[2]

The serious note of the ode on the *Miseres de l'homme* does
not in fact predominate in the collections of poems published
by Ronsard between 1554 and 1556. On the contrary, the tone
of these so-called anacreontic poems (inspired by Henri
Estienne's discovery of the pseudo-Anacreon, a manuscript he
published himself in 1554) is in the main light-hearted. They
are rustic *odelettes,* featuring the *repas champêtre.*[3] Evidently
nature still interests the poet but she is more static and the
movement of these poems follows the conventional pattern,
emphasized by the use of present participles in the antique
manner, of diminutives and by the general tone of *mignardise.*[4]
This style is above all literary and pretentious, emphasizing as
it does the mythological anecdote, learning and a precious
type of decoration. The desire for technical achievement over-

---

[1] Laum., vol. V, p. 192 (*Ode sur les miseres des hommes*), and vol. VI,
p. 10 (*Epitre,* later called *Sur les plaisirs rustiques*).

[2] Cf. especially the paradoxes of O. Lassi, translated and published many
times by C. Estienne towards the middle of the century.

[3] Cf. Laum., vol. VI, pp. 106, 175, 238 and so on.

[4] Cf. Laum., vol. VII, p. 141, note 2.

comes the love element as well as the natural element. Even
the *Folastries* had been called by Magny *doctes folies*:[1] how
much more learned were these *odelettes* with their advertised
sources, where the *avette* becomes the *serpenteau ailé*, where
Cupid is invariably *méchant* and where both reader and poet
are hopelessly involved in an over-elaborate piece of rococo.[2]
There is progress in the technical field. The decorative *motifs*
which abound in these poems are less clumsy, even if they are
less full of joy and movement. The meals themselves, eaten as
they are in rustic surroundings, are very different from the
exuberant picnic of the *Voyage d'Hercueil*[3] and the poet seems
to be in danger of becoming lost in a mass of over-delicate
preciosities. Gone is the sensuality and coarseness of the
pindaric odes and much of their vitality. Ronsard laments the
departure of youth and the greying of his hair.[4] R. Belleau, in
a commentary, suggests that this new style is meant by Ronsard as a *tour de force* to show that: 'il sçait bien escrimer à
toutes mains du baston qu'il manie', [5] but, although many of
these affectations are delightful,[6] the poet produces a sense of
emptiness in the reader at times and the genre is perhaps too
small to hold the care and polish lavished upon it.

Despite a number of pleasant and unstilted phrases, we are
very conscious of the standard pattern of rhetoric underlying
the ode: *Quand je suis vint ou trente mois...*,[7] with its firm
statement of the theme expanded in successive verses, each
dealing with one of the aspects proposed, the whole neatly

[1] Cf. Laumonier: *Ronsard, poète lyrique*, p. 103.

[2] Contrast his *Amour mouillé* with that of La Fontaine.

[3] As the poet says: 'Je hai tant de viandes' (Laum., vol. II, p. 47). Cf. also
vol. VII, p. 106, and compare these menus with those advocated by Ficino
(*Les trois livres de la vie*) (translated by G. Lefèvre de la Boderie, Paris, 1581),
p. 18.

[4] Laum., vol. VII, p. 102.

[5] Laum., vol. X, p. xxii.

[6] Cf. Laum., vol. VII, p. 139.

[7] Cf. Appendix, p. 134.

tied up and snapped off in the last stanza. This ode is the climax of the poet's striving for a *classical* order with a beginning (exposition of themes), middle (development of themes proposed) and end (the commonplace conclusion which relates the particular to the general): it is the most coherent and eloquent example of the 'logical' order, one which is to become more and more rare in Ronsard's poetry after the late 1550's. It can readily be compared with *Bel aubepin...*,[1] that other masterpiece of nature description published at this time. This poem retains much more of the *blason*, but any suggestion that it harks back to the technique of linear digression, or even that it has a great deal in common with such poems as Corrozet's *Blason du jardin*, is obviously absurd. The poem is organized quite differently, around a convention which is much more fragile and which is cleverly, almost finickily neoclassical in its delicacy.

It must be said that *Quand je suis...* is even more closely and centrally organized and that it can, in fact, be seen as a sort of illustrated commonplace, revolving around one or more generalities. It is however saved from reproach by the subtleties of harmony, the varied rhythms and the use of sound in general which enchants the reader and causes him to discount the apparently over-organized nature of the structure.

The *Amours de Marie* (as they were later called), published in 1555–6, are not the exact counterpart of these anacreontic *odelettes*. They can better be situated by contrasting them with the sonnets dedicated to Cassandre in 1552, when their peculiar simplicity becomes apparent. Two sonnets will serve as an example:

> Quand au matin ma Deesse s'abille
> D'un riche or crespe ombrageant ses talons,

---

[1] Cf. Appendix, p. 136.

Et que les retz de ses beaulx cheveux blondz
En cent façons ennonde & entortille:
  Je l'acompare à l'escumiere fille,
Qui or peignant les siens jaunement longz,
Or les ridant en mille crespillons
Nageoyt abord dedans une coquille.

  De femme humaine encore ne sont pas
Son ris, son front, ses gestes, ny ses pas,
Ny de ses yeulx l'une & l'autre chandelle:
  Rocz, eaux, ny boys, ne celent point en eulx
Nymphe, qui ait si follastres cheveux,
Ny l'œil si beau, ny la bouche si belle.

  Mignongne, levés-vous, vous estes paresseuse,
Ja la gaye alouette au ciel a fredonné,
Et ja le rossignol frisquement jargonné,
Dessus l'espine assis, sa complainte amoureuse.

  Debout donq, allon voir l'herbelette perleuse,
Et vostre beau rosier de boutons couronné,
Et voz œillets aimés, ausquels avés donné
Hyer au soir de l'eau, d'une main si songneuse.

  Hyer en vous couchant, vous me fistes promesse
D'estre plus-tost que moi ce matin eveillée,
Mais le someil vous tient encor toute sillée:

  Ian, je vous punirai du peché de paresse,
Je vois baiser cent fois vostre œil, vostre tetin,
Afin de vous aprendre à vous lever matin.[1]

The difference is mainly one of tone. Both are *aubades*, making use of convention, although the conventions are widely different. The first sonnet introduces us into a neo-Italian rather than a neoclassical world: the poet's mistress is a goddess, she clothes herself in rich gold and her hair is waved and twisted in the manner of an Italian Renaissance

[1] Laum., vol. IV, p. 42, and vol. VII, p. 140. A further *aubade* to Cassandre is to be found: Laum., vol. IV, p. 79.

picture. As a goddess inspiring love, she is naturally compared with Venus, and this is the excuse for a rich, sensual but naïve picture of Venus who 'nageoyt abord dedans une coquille'. Finally, she is declared to be a Nymph and situated in imagination in a sketchily Petrarchan landscape.

The conventions of the second sonnet are more rustic. The *alouette*, the *rossignol*, the *rosier* and the *œillets* all play their role, and the poet's mistress is a country lover rather than a goddess; she is scarcely voluptuous, certainly not fashionable, and is even represented as a gardener and a waterer of flowers.

Yet, although we may suggest a partial return to the opinion of earlier critics who regarded the Marie poems as more simple than those addressed to Cassandre, we must not exaggerate the rusticity of these later poems. Although the similes from the jeweller's shop-window which are so frequent in 1552 have, on the whole, given way to metaphors from the countryside, the 1555–6 poems retain much of the artificiality of the *mignardise*:

> Marie, vous avés la joue aussi vermeille
> Qu'une rose de Mai, vous avés les cheveus
> De couleur de chastaigne, entrefrisés de neus,
> Gentement tortillés tout-au-tour de l'oreille.
>
> Quand vous estiés petite, une mignarde abeille
> Dans vos levres forma son dous miel savoureus,
> Amour laissa ses traits dans vos yeus rigoreus,
> Pithon vous feit la vois à nulle autre pareille.
>
> Vous avés les tetins comme deux mons de lait,
> Caillé bien blanchement sus du jonc nouvelet
> Qu'une jeune pucelle au mois de Juin façonne:
>
> De Junon sont vos bras, des Graces vostre sein,
> Vous avés de l'Aurore & le front, & la main,
> Mais vous avés le cœur d'une fiere lionne.[1]

---

[1] Laum., vol. VII, p. 126. It is interesting to compare the original version of this sonnet, in which the poet sticks to a *local* metaphor—a certain girl

The Petrarchan obsession with love and with solitude continues, but perhaps the landscapes where the poet walks
thinking of his love are less mysterious and wild than in 1552.[1]

If we are to define the atmosphere of the nature descriptions
of this period, we may do so by drawing on the scholarship of
M. Desonay, who has gathered together a number of examples
showing Ronsard's attachment to the word *douceur* at this
time.[2] Certainly this word might well be applied to such descriptions as the *Bel aubepin*, and with it we are very far from
the Ronsard of the pindaric odes. The secrets whispered by
daimons in the ear of the poet seem to have vanished and this
poetry has become pleasant and easy-flowing rather than didactic. The Nymphs are invoked rather than the Muses, and
then rather casually.[3] The moral of the poem, if there be one,
is a means towards unity rather than a centre of interest, and
we are almost in the type of atmosphere which greets the
reader at the beginning of the *Roman de la Rose*.[4] In fact, from
a deliberately emphatic conception of the poet as a prophet
impelled and oppressed by fury and devoted to the indirect
expression of the secrets of the universe, Ronsard seems to
have become the contented author of a series of respectable
classical compositions. He has brought the technique of description from the primitive list through the *blason* of the
earlier part of the century (a technique reflected in those of his

---

at a certain time making cheese by a certain method, with later ones in which
the text is much more generalized: cf. the variants given by Laumonier.

[1] Cf. Laum., vol. VII, pp. 184, 144.

[2] F. Desonay: *Ronsard, poète de l'amour*, vol. II, p. 122. Most of these
examples come from the *Elégie à Choiseul*, published in 1556.

[3] Cf. Laum., vol. VI, p. 137.

[4] Cf. lines 603–6:

> Maintes foix pour s'esbaneier
> Se vient en cest leu ombreier
> Deduiz e les genz qui le sivent,
> Qui en joie e en solaz vivent.

1550 odes which describe certain aspects of the *Vendômois*) to
the Ronsardian *blason* as defined by M. Raymond,[1] which is
indeed an excuse to tell a mythological fable, to which the
title of the poem is related and which becomes the centre of
interest, and finally to the poem, *Bel aubepin*, which is basic-
ally a *blason*, but which contains little of the clumsiness of the
list type of poem, although structurally, of course, it is
developed from it.

All this he has achieved through *imitation* (as in the
Fontaine Bellerie) and by adaptation, as in *Quand je suis vint
ou trente mois...* of the *classical* order of formal composition.
In what can be seen as a struggle towards order and legitimacy
he has, by 1556, tried most of the poetic genres advised by the
Deffence et Illustration: the ode, the *odelette*, the sonnet, the
hymn, the *blason*, the elegy, the pastoral and even a type of
epic in such poems as the *Hymne de Pollux et de Castor*.[2] Also
—and this is more important—he has stated certain themes.
He has described the detail of nature (*natura naturata*) and has
given the reader a glimpse not merely of the laws of Nature,
but of the cosmic powers summed up in the concept of
natura naturans. This he has done particularly in the constantly recurring picture of the *Bal des Nymphes*, *Danse des
Muses* and so on, which appear to be a symbol of cosmic
roundness and the recurrence of phenomena in a universe
whose order is predominantly cyclic.

Ronsard is considered to be a lyric poet. This is exact if we
use the word in the sense suggested by Desonay: 'Mouvement
égale lyrisme: nous en revenons toujours là'.[3] Yet, up to 1556,
this lyricism has scarcely shown itself to be personal, except

---

[1] *L'influence de Ronsard* (Paris, 1927), vol. I, p. 153.
[2] Laum., vol. VIII, p. 293.
[3] F. Desonay: *Ronsard, poète de l'amour*, vol. I, p. 90.

in so far as any style of writing must bear this puzzling and inexact description. What have we, so far, which belongs to Ronsard specifically? Descriptions of the *Vendômois*, where the poet spent much of his youth, a number of love poems which can by no means be guaranteed to be the expression of personal feelings, a statement of certain autobiographical facts, addressed to Pierre Paschal and intended for a particular purpose,[1] and finally, in his nature poetry, the description of certain details and sites, some known and apparently loved, some imagined or imitated.

This type of description continues after 1556, but the *vignette-mignardise* of the new style begins to develop into the comparison, or we may call it simply the *description*, using this term as it is defined by Ramus in a work to which Ronsard certainly had access:

> Or cette succinte breveté n'est pas perpetuelle en ceste espece: mais souvent & la chose & l'auditeur requiert explication plus illustre & magnifique: comme sont presques les descriptions des poëtes. Telles sont souvent les descriptions des plantes, arbres & animaux es philosophes, & celles des villes, fleuves, montaignes es historiens. Et comme la breveté est louée en la parfaite definition, ainsi la magnificence est celebrée en la description: moyennant toutesfois qu'il n'y ayt rien de superflu.[2]

The same kind of *description*, obviously decorative in its effect, had occurred in Ronsard's pindaric odes: in fact the word *pindariser* is used even by Lemaire de Belges in 1513[3] to suggest an elevated, even an inflated type of poetry. And

---

[1] Cf. Laum., vol. VI, p. 61.

[2] P. Ramus: *Dialectique* (Paris, 1555), pp. 59-60. On this point cf. also some remarks on the *amplificatio* by P. Zumthor in: *Euphémisme et rhétorique au Moyen âge* (*Cahiers de l'Association internationale des études françaises*, Nos. 3-4-5, July 1953, p. 177).

[3] *Concorde*, line 281 (ed. J. Frappier, p. 19).

although, in his Hymns, Ronsard does not entirely forsake
the humble comparison:

> Comme un fromage mol, qui surpendu s'égoute
> Par les trous d'un pannier, à terre goute à goute.[1]

he concentrates upon the majestic, the exciting and even the
horrible, as can be seen from the following passage from the
Hymne de Calaïs, et de Zetes:

> Criailler d'un grand bruict, comme on oit dans un bois
> Pres le bord de la Mer crier l'horrible voix
> Des Palles & Butors, quand un larron ils trouvent
> Qui remarque leur nic, & leurs femmes qui couvent.
> Puis tout soudainement sans les appercevoir
> (Comme un fouldre d'esté qui pront se laisse choir)
> Vollants du haut du ciel dessus luy se percherent,
> Et de leurs becs crochus la viande arracherent
> Hors de ses vuides mains, haletant une odeur
> Qui empuantissoit des Chevalliers le cœur.[2]

Decorative as they are, such comparisons seem, however,
designed to be something more. They are undoubtedly
intended to make the reader feel noble, stirred, occasionally
calm. In fact they follow out one of the precepts of the
Deffence et Illustration:

> celuy sera veritablement le poëte que je cherche en nostre
> Langue, qui me fera indigner, apayser, ejouyr, douloir, aymer,
> hayr, admirer, etonner, bref, qui tiendra la bride de mes affec-
> tions, me tournant ça et la à son plaisir.[3]

The best of Ronsard's set comparisons or *descriptions* then
reinforce the text emotionally[4] much in the same way as the
classical device of *amplification* 'raises acts and personal traits

---

[1] Laum., vol. VIII, p. 153.   [2] Ibid., p. 274.
[3] *Deffence et Illustration*, p. 179.
[4] Cf. the series used in the *Institution pour l'adolescence du Roy* (Laum.,
vol. XI, pp. 3 ff.).

above their real dimensions'.[1] Is this also true of the comparisons which form so great a part of the text of Ronsard's epic,
the *Franciade*?

The preface to this poem (published between 1572 and
1587) suggests that in fact these comparisons are the main
preoccupation of the poet:

> un bon artisan, qui les face autant qu'il luy sera possible hausser,
> comme les peintures relevees, & quasi separer du langage
> commun, les ornant & enrichissant de Figures, Schemes, Tropes,
> Metaphores, Phrases & periphrases eslongnees presque du tout,
> ou pour le moins separees, de la prose triviale & vulgaire.

And again:

> Tu enrichiras ton Poëme par varietez prises de la Nature...
> Souvienne toy, Lecteur, de ne laisser passer soubs silence... la
> nature, force, & proprietez des arbres, fleurs, plantes & racines...
> Tu n'oubliras aussi ny les montaignes, forests, rivieres...
> cavernes & rochers... pour embellir ton œuvre par là.

We seem in fact to see here a further manifestation of the
influence of Virgil: Ronsard wishes the poets to write 'leurs
conceptions d'un style nombreux, plein d'une venerable
majesté, comme a faict Virgile en sa divine *Æneide*' and he
suggests that his poem is 'enrichi[es] de passements, broderies,
tapisseries, et entrelassements de fleurs poëtiques'.[2]

Certainly the *Franciade* is full of comparisons taken from
noble aspects of nature: lions, falcons, lightnings and eagles are
easily to be found. But there are also descriptions of more
humble creatures, particularly of birds:

> Autant qu'on voit dans les creux marescages
> Du bas Poitou, oyseaux de tous plumages,

---

[1] Note the difference between this and medieval amplification which 'simply
indicates . . . the purely linear extension, expansion, unrolling of a theme'
(Curtius: *European literature*, p. 492).

[2] Laum., vol. XVI, pp. 332, 334, 340, 341, 338, 332.

Maretz bourbeux, limoneux, & tramblants,...
Qui s'esgayant en leurs æsles se jouënt:
Les uns sur l'eau, les autres au fond nouënt,...
Autres plus bas sur les rives connues
Soubs les rouseaux, ou souz l'ombre des joncs,
Oyes, canars, & cygnes aux cols longs
Estandent l'æsle, & s'esplument, & crient,
Qui haut qui bas: les rivages en bruient![1]

The poem itself does indeed move from one matter to
another 'en cent sortes de varietez'.[2] It is splendid and magnificent in its descriptions. Yet the action itself is jerky. Francus
and his career rapidly fade from view behind a mass of
continually moving scenery. The combat between Francus
and the giant Phovère is of no greater importance poetically
than the time of day, declared in the Virgilian manner:

Incontinent que l'Aube aux doigs de roses
Eut du grand ciel les barrieres décloses,
Versant les fleurs sur les yeux du Soleil,
Rouge tantost, tantost jaune & vermeil,
Se bigarrant en autant de manieres
Qu'on voit fleurir les rives printanieres:
Le Roy Dicæe...[3]

And even the seeker after poetry concerning nature is puzzled
by the technical and realistic description of the cutting of the
wood for the building of the ships. Such passages are perhaps
designed to connect the marvellous in the story with the
observed world at least as much as to stimulate the imagination
of the reader.

Yet many Ronsardian descriptions depend upon the fantasy
and the imagination for their very existence. This is especially
true of later poems, when the *description* has merged into the

[1] Laum., vol. XVI, p. 73. Cf. also p. 90.   [2] Ibid., p. 343.
[3] Ibid., p. 116.

poème, defined as follows by Ronsard in a poem published after his death:

> Poëme et Poësie ont grande difference.
> Poësie est un pré de diverse apparence,
> Orgueilleux de ses biens et riche de ses fleurs,
> Diapré, peinturé de cent mille couleurs,
> Qui fournist de bouquets les amantes pucelles,
> Et de vivres les camps des abeilles nouvelles.
> Poëme est une fleur, ou comme en des forés
> Un seul chesne, un seul orme, un sapin, un cyprés,
> Qu'un nerveux charpentier tourne en courbes charrues,
> Ou en carreaux voutez des navires ventrues,...[1]

Among the *Poemes* of 1569 are one or two examples of the *blason* become *poème*. In *Le Pin*,[2] for example, a particular pine tree in Ronsard's garden has a fable built round it, and this is followed by a somewhat laborious and forbidding explanation which makes the transition from the particular to the general.

This generalization of particular phenomena is a characteristic which does not belong exclusively to his later poems. Nowhere does he represent the forces behind reality and nature more lightly and yet with more gravely precise symbolism than in the constantly recurring pictures of the dance of the Nymphs or the Muses.[3] That this, for Ronsard's contemporaries, is a serious symbol of the workings of a cyclic Nature[4] is indicated in a little-known work by Bérenger de La

---

[1] Cohen, vol. II, p. 662.   [2] Laum., vol. XV, p. 178.

[3] Cf. among other refs.: Laum., vol. III, pp. 81, 82, 99, 167; vol. IV, pp. 4, 137; vol. VI, p. 112; vol. VII, pp. 75, 109; vol. VIII, pp. 78, 151, 161. Ronsard also refers to the *bal des étoiles* (cf. Laum., vol. VIII, p. 91) and the dance or *sabbat* of the *daimons* (Laum., vol. VIII, p. 134). Cf. also Laum., vol. VII, p. 109, note 6.

[4] Laumonier, however, tells us that the *cottes* of these dancing Nymphs are the mists that rise in the evening over the *Vendômois* meadows. But, whatever the value of this suggestion in certain instances, we must recognize that, for the poet, these creatures replace the realities of nature which he undoubtedly

Tour: *Choréide, Autrement, Louenge du bal* (Lyons, 1556) in
which dancing is represented as a kind of worship of the
spheres:

> Les Cieus ont esté les premiers,
> Et seront aussi les derniers,
> Qui ont dansé, et danseront...
> Le feu... ne fait il
> Danser les flammes?...
> Et pour aus animaus descendre
> Qui les pourroit au milieu fandre,
> Il verroit un bal ordinaire
> Au polmon, au cœur, en l'artere...
> Le bal est le propre de l'ame;...[1]

As we see, the whole idea of movement is, according to
Ronsard and to the neoplatonists, one principle of that vague
concept, the *soul*. Thus, to describe it is to convey not merely
an impression of an object—it is in some way to convey its
essence, and this is why the type of description and the poetic
image particularly favoured by Ronsard are continually ex-
pressive of maturation, of movement, of life. The poem, or at
all events the single natural description, is worked around a
central *motif*, frequently a symbol. Movement (and often a
vaguely circular movement as in dancing) pervades the poem,
and not only what is described but the way in which it is
described partakes of this movement. Desonay insists con-
vincingly that the lyrical and the musical are forms of
controlled movement, of poetic rhythm:

Dans la querelle qui opposa Budé à Camerarius concernant le

---

observed. The imagination dominates and overwhelms the memory, and the
object itself takes second place to the feeling it evokes in the poet. (Cf. Laum.,
vol. XII, p. 48, note 2.)

[1] This is not perhaps the normal attitude of the century towards dancing,
as witness: *Le Blason des danses où se voyent les malheurs et ruines venant des
danses. . . .* (G. Paradin, Beaujeu, 1556).

sens à donner à l'entéléchie aristotélicienne, Ronsard, ne craig-
nons pas d'y insister, est pour le mouvement cher à Platon.
Mouvement égale lyrisme: nous en revenons toujours là. Les
allusions néoplatoniciennes des *Amours*: ou les manifestations
d'un tempérament poétique dont le mouvement passionné est
la loi.[1]

Indeed, there are passages in which Ronsard describes that
which has never existed, and here the movement is somewhat
different. He takes refuge from the Court and from ambition
in the *Vendômois*, but also in pictures of the Golden Age and
the *Isles fortunées*, whose restful languor he conveys so well
in 1555.[2] And, although he describes the *Vendômois* often
enough with a topographical exactitude which is impressive,
as at the beginning of the *Voyage de Tours*,[3] his best descriptions of that region are by no means always as exact.
Here, unreality appears particularly in the form of mythology,
as in the case of the dance of the Nymphs discussed above.

The basic reasons for the employment of mythology by
sixteenth-century writers in France appear in two statements,
one by Lemaire de Belges and one by Charles Fontaine.
Lemaire includes in his *Illustrations de Gaule* a long description of the combat between Paris and Menelaus:

> laquelle est diffusément narre par le prince des poetes Homere...
> et bien couloures de fleurs poetiques... je vueil icy marrester
> ung petit a descrire ledit combat pource qu'il est beau et delect-
> able et sent bien son antiquite...[4]

Charles Fontaine says in 1545:

> en l'esprit [du poète] y a tousjours je ne sçay quoy de gayeté
> naturelle, sans laquelle (j'ose dire) ne se peult appeler Poëte.

---

[1] F. Desonay: *Ronsard, poète de l'amour*, vol. I, p. 90.
[2] Laum., vol. V, p. 182.
[3] Laum., vol. X, p. 215.
[4] *Illustrations*, Book II, Chap. XVI (Stecher, p. 152).

E

Et de là vient que anciennement les Poëtes ont feint, & inventé plusieurs choses plaisantes, pour avoir matière, et occasion d'escrire: comme des Nymphes des boys, des fleurs, des fleuves, des neuf Muses qui s'entretiennent par la main et dansent sur la verdure... de Bacchus tousjours jeune & joyeux, de Venus, de Cupido, de Pan, des Faunes & Satyres, qui ont avecq' eulx quelques voluptez et lascivetez non à despriser en Poësie.[1]

Thus Lemaire loves mythology because it introduces a breath of antiquity, because it embodies learning, and also perhaps because it is generally embellished with poetic flowers. Charles Fontaine loves it because it is pleasant and lively. We have seen that Ronsard goes further than either of these poets. According to Professor Seznec, 'la mythologie confuse, indigeste, dont il s'est gorgé, n'étouffe pas son imagination; elle l'enivre, elle l'exalte, car il y sent frémir l'âme éparse de la nature'.[2] Certainly it is rare to find a description of nature in Ronsard's poetry in which we do not discover demigods, satyrs and even fairies. He does not immediately find himself a master of the technique of using mythological figures and fables. The coarse figures of the *Avant-venue du Printemps* and the clumsy rituals of the *De l'election de son sepulcre* take some time to develop into the involved but delicate periphrases of the *Hymne de l'Automne*, and the conventions of the first odes describing the Forest of *Gâtine* become only at the end of Ronsard's career the

[1] In the preface to his *Fontaine d'amour* (Paris, 1545).

[2] J. Seznec: *La survivance des dieux antiques* (London, 1940), p. 275. Only rarely does Ronsard use mythology as a simple metonymy as in the definition given by Fouquelin in 1555: 'Metonomie est un Trope, par le quel la diction trouvée & instituée pour signifier proprement la cause de quelque chose que ce soit, est mise & usurpée pour signifier l'effet... Par cette maniére souvente-fois ce mot (Ceres) signifiant la déesse qui a premierement trouvé les fruictz, est mis & usurpé pour les fruictz mémes. Ronsart en l'Hymne de France:

> Plus qu'en nul lieu dame Ceres la blonde,
> Et le donteur des Indes y abonde' (p. 2).

artificial evocation of the *Bûcheron* elegy. This elegy on the
cutting down of part of the *Forêt de Gâtine*,[1] published by
Ronsard in 1584, begins with an antique fable and ends with
a *sentence*, proof perhaps of the didactic intention of the poet
and an adequate frame for the description of the forest itself
which occupies most of the rest of the poem. Ronsard seems
to have no use for 'facts' and for the normal vocabulary of
forest description. Quite early in the poem we see the phrase:
'le sang de nos forests', and this sets the tone for what is to
follow. It is not the forest itself which is to be described, but
the life which inhabits it, not the various sorts of trees but the
spirit of the wood:

> Ce ne sont pas des bois que tu jettes à bas,
> Ne vois-tu pas le sang, lequel degoute à force
> Des Nymphes qui vivoyent dessous la dure escorce?[2]

We then pass from the Nymphs—who, despite their classical
origins, are treated in a very unclassical fashion—to the more
normal inhabitants of the wood:

> Forest, haute maison des oiseaux bocagers,
> Plus le cerf solitaire et les chevreuls legers
> Ne paistront sous ton ombre,...

Each of these creatures is denoted by one simple but telling
adjective: 'le cerf solitaire' sums up in his attitude the whole
feeling of the forest.

  The life of the trees is again emphasized in the phrase: 'ta
verte criniere', and then the poet slows down this movement,
beginning his picture of peace and silence with a four-line

---

[1] Cohen, vol. II, p. 116 (Appendix, p. 15 f.).
[2] For other uses of this same picture, cf. Laum., vol. VI, p. 142; vol. XV,
p. 178. Also Laum., vol. VII, p. 109.

evocation of the pastoral state, followed by three lines of gentle, calm pulsation:

> Tout deviendra muet, Echo sera sans voix,
> Tu deviendras campagne, et, en lieu de tes bois,
> Dont l'ombrage incertain lentement se remue,...

Into this vision of peace there is then injected a further three lines, connected by the rhyme:

> Tu sentiras le soc, le coutre et la charrue.
> Tu perdras ton silence, et, haletans d'effroy,
> Ny Satyres, ny Pans ne viendront plus chez toy.

Here the sound, indeed the noise, of the lines presents a real and apparent picture, even down to the use of imitative harmony. And the poet says farewell to the 'vieille forest, le jouet de Zephyre', invoking the antique figures of poetry-making: *Apollon*, *Calliope* and *Euterpe*, before ending the elegy on the note of general didacticism and the philosophy of change.

Ronsard has in fact accomplished the *tour de force* of describing, or rather evoking, a forest with scarcely any *real* detail. Only a few phrases suggest the physical aspects of the wood: 'la dure escorce', 'ta verte criniere' and the gentle movement implied in: 'Dont l'ombrage incertain lentement se remue' and 'le frais de tes douces verdures'. The rest of the poem, taking its note from the first compelling image of the bleeding Nymphs, mingles mythology, sound, the pastoral convention and the contrast between quiet and calm inhabited by forces which are part of the *nature* of the wood to produce a poem which brings before the reader the general in the guise of the particular, and atmosphere and emotion in the guise of description.

CHAPTER III

Nature as Controlling Force

natura naturans

THE clearest and most comprehensive definition of Nature in French during the Renaissance is probably that in Gohorry's translation of the extremely popular work by Lemnius: *Les occultes merveilles et secretz de nature*:

> Nature est une qualité infuse és choses des leur commencement & naissance. Nature est temperature & mixtion des quatre elemens. Nature est l'instinct & inclination de l'esprit d'un chascun. Aux Philosophes nature est le commencement du mouvement & du repos. Nature est celle qui donne forme à toute chose selon sa speciale difference.[1] Nature est la vertu & cause efficiente & conservative de toutes choses: laquelle est inseree en tout le monde. Nature... est l'ordre & continuation des œuvres divines: laquelle obeit à sa puissance & à ses paroles & commandemens, & d'iceluy emprunte ses forces.[2]

The part of this definition which concerns the central power of an all-controlling Nature reappears in the dialogues of Le Caron:

> Car nature ne se propose, que de rendre perfait et accompli ce

Cf. Scholastic notions of *form*. These notions are perhaps more relevant to Montaigne (cf. his ideas of *maistresse-forme*, etc.) than to Ronsard. However, they can be related to the meanings of *nature* seen here in Chapters III and IV.

[2] L. Lemnius (Paris, 154), p. 6.

qu'elle procree: et partout elle s'eforce de composer châcune chose en tel ordre et convenance de ses parties, qu'on ne puisse trouver quelque defaut ne messeance en sa disposition et agensement.[1]

He goes on to say that the force which holds together the various parts of the universe in this way is:

quelque chose laquelle j'ai oui diversement appeller, maintenant la providence divine, maintenant l'ame du monde, quelque fois nature.

An apparently simple account of Nature and one of the earliest definitions in French of the phrases *natura naturata* and *natura naturans* is given in the *Cœur de philosophie*,[2] a sixteenth-century adaptation of a fourteenth-century 'philosophic' dialogue:

Placides je vous dy que deux manieres de nature sont. La prem-iere si est appellee nature naturant & lautre nature naturee. Nature naturant si est telle nature parquoy toutes natures sont faictes & dont toutes autres natures sont soustenues. Et nature naturee si sont toutes les choses qui sont dessoubz nature & en plusieurs manieres fut jadis nommee & est encores nature naturant. Jacoit ce que la premiere cause que nous appellons dieu ne puisse estre nommee... Ce sont les deux natures qui sont ne plus nen est / mais en maintes manieres sont divisees les natures / Car ce sont toutes les choses qui sont soubz Dieu qui toutes estoient ensemble avant que generation fuct faicte que Dieu qui est generation divisa en maintes manieres soubz soy.

This division of nature is a usual and convenient one.[3] In

---

[1] L. Le Caron: *Dialogues*, f. 154.

[2] We quote from the edition published by Philippe le Noir at the begin-ning of the century (1520). Other early editions possessed by the *Bibliothèque Nationale* fail to clear up the obvious difficulties in the text itself.

[3] Cf. L. Le Roy's commentary on Plato's *Timée* (Paris, 1551), which presents the same picture in slightly different terms, using in fact the termino-logy of Plutarch:

'Plutarque dit que la nature mesme n'est autre chose, que l'idee des choses

this chapter we shall deal more particularly with *natura naturans*, Nature as the controlling power which is behind the irregular movements, the *va-et-vient*, the antithetical and contrary forces which appear in the sublunar universe, the power which prevents this flux from degenerating into chaos, imposing upon the details of creation certain laws which tend towards rhythm (usually cyclic) and equilibrium.

This aspect of nature is emphasized in Ronsard's 'scientific' poetry and especially in the Hymns which he published in 1555 and 1556. Just as the idea of a world in flux is not incompatible with the idea of a type of *spiritus* or *âme du monde* working within and controlling all things, so indeed the idea of control by Nature is not incompatible with the idea of a master-control, an over-riding power which is God.[1] As Ronsard says himself:

> Car la Nature & Dieu est presque chose mesme:
> Dieu commande partout comme Prince absolu,
> Elle execute & fait cela qu'il a voulu,
> Son ordre est une chesne aimantine & ferree.[2]

As far as Ronsard is concerned, it would appear that his interest shifts, about 1555, from the straightforward description of the details of nature to a more general interest in Nature as a power behind the universe, which he begins to

---

qui sont tousjours semblables: & l'autre ou diverse, l'idee de celles qui reçoyvent continuele difference: l'office de l'une estre de separer, alterer, & multiplier: de l'autre, assembler, & de plusieurs en faire un, par la similitude qu'ils ont ensemble' (*Timée*, f. 30).

[1] In the *Roman de la Rose* this is expressed very simply: Nature is the *chambriere* of God and the universe. That sixteenth-century writers in general shared this view or a similar one is suggested by H. Busson: *Sources et développement du rationalisme* (Paris, 1922), p. 255, by J. E. Du Monin: *Nouvelles Œuvres* (Paris, 1581), p. 70, in a poem dedicated to Ronsard, by L. Le Caron: *Dialogues* (Paris, 1556), ff. 83, 91, etc., and, of course, by Ronsard himself.

[2] Laum., vol. XVII, p. 80. These lines were published posthumously.

feel as a whole. This shift of interest from the particular and unconnected to the general and unified seems to find a parallel in the style of his work. He ceases to be content to describe (frequently almost in *blason* form) the separate details of nature. Even in the early pindaric odes, the poet had described occasionally the harmony of the extralunar universe, notably in a number of pictures of night and the stars and in the indirect symbol of the dance of the demigods. He now begins to discover and express the laws of nature which weld sublunar phenomena into a whole.

These laws appear, somewhat monotonously perhaps, in a number of poems published in 1553 and 1554. Laumonier even goes so far as to hint at a 'crise de mélancolie' in the poet's life at this time, but these passages scarcely seem to correspond to any single state of mind on the part of the poet. Furthermore, they are very directly tendentious and usually heavily weighted on the side of sorrow or of joy.[1]

Such poems, however, are almost on the fringe of the question and it is to the Hymns of 1555 and 1556 that we must go in order to find the most complete picture of the cosmos according to Ronsard.

Ronsard's first book of Hymns was published only just after Peletier du Mans' collection of neoplatonic and scientific poetry, the *Amour des Amours*, which appeared early in 1555 according to Chamard.[2] These two adventures in the world of cosmic poetry afford fascinating points of comparison and of difference.[3] Whereas Ronsard proposes a review of the

---

[1] Cf. the pair of poems addressed to Ambroise de la Porte (Laum., vol. V, p. 192, and vol. VI, p. 10). For a possible theory of this type of verse cf. *Deffence et Illustration*, pp. 56, 112.

[2] *Histoire de la Pléiade*, vol. II, p. 131.

[3] For the relations between the two poets at this time, cf. P. Laumonier's introduction to Peletier's *Art poétique* (ed. A. Boulanger, Paris, 1930), pp. 23 ff.

whole of scientific knowledge in his *Hymne de la Philosophie*:

> Elle premiere a trouvé l'ouverture
> Par long travail des secretz de Nature,
> A sçeu de quoy les tonnerres se font,
> Pourquoy la Lune a maintenant le front
> Mousse, ou cornu, & pourquoy toute ronde
> Ou demi-ronde elle apparoist au Monde,
> A sçeu pourquoy le Soleil perd couleur,...[1]

Peletier is not content with similar vague, orphic generalities. He studies the mechanism of the sublunar universe and devotes several poems to meteorology, as for example *La Rosée*,[2] a poem which makes a convenient contrast with Ronsard's Hymns in its minute and, it must be said, unpoetical analysis of a physical phenomenon. Ronsard is writing as a poet rather than as a scientist or even as one wishing to reveal Nature and her powers to others. His views on the universe do not find expression in a creed, perhaps because they are not fixed. On none of the controversial questions of his time does he take a stand; he maintains no firm belief in any one attitude, for neither belief nor doctrine is at the focal point of any of his Hymns.

Even so, the universe he describes is the standard universe of the Renaissance (and indeed of the Middle Ages), based upon the fundamental distinction between an extralunar world, in which all is stability and harmony, and a sublunar world, in which all is flux and depends upon stress and equilibrium between elemental forces.[3] In his Hymns, Ronsard focuses our attention now upon the sublunar (in the *Hymne des Daimons* and the *Hymne de la Mort*), now upon the extralunar (in the *Hymne du Ciel*, the *Hymne de l'Eternité* and the

---

[1] Laum., vol. VIII, p. 90.
[2] *Amour des Amours*, p. 79.
[3] Cf. Ronsard's epitaph for Blondet (Laum., vol. X, p. 308).

Hymne des Astres).[1] Of these two regions, man inhabits the one and, especially if he is a neoplatonist, aspires to the other. Yet none of these Hymns deals specifically with this aspiration. This may be because Ronsard's ideas at this time are un-developed and indeed largely unformed. He is ready to give us a picture—again almost in the form of a *blason*—of certain phenomena, but he is not ready to put any doctrine before us.

The *Hymne de la Mort* offers a convenient example of this hesitancy, although the elegant languor of the introductory lines, with their note of conventional hypocrisy, bears no sign of hesitation[2] and the calm verses of the first development— that Death is in fact a happy release from a laborious world full of *peine*—throw a most unusual light upon the conven-tional picture of a stable, harmonious, extralunar world:

> Mais le Soleil, la Lune, & les Astres des Cieux
> Font avecque travail leur tour laborieux:...[3]

The poet comes down to earth, and adds more detail of a conventional nature to his picture of a temporal existence, contrasting the broken byways of this world with the straight path of Death, whose calm power is apparently soothing and healing when we reach her *hostel*.

Here, however, with the reader already persuaded and quiescent, Ronsard introduces a further opinion, that of another school of thinkers who, despite their stated wrong-headedness, employ a most convincing turn of phrase:

> Beaucoup ne sçachans point, qu'ilz sont enfans de Dieu,
> Pleurent avant partir, & s'atristent au lieu
> De chanter hautement le Pëan de victoire,
> Et pensent que la Mort soit quelque beste noire,

---

[1] Laum., vol. VIII, pp. 115, 161, 140, 246, 150.   [2] Ibid., p. 163 e.s.

[3] Ibid., p. 165. Cf. the source of these lines—Virgil (*Georgics*, II, 478). We should note that, later in the poem, the travail of the heavens is related to the infinite calm of God.

> Qui les viendra manger, & que dix mille vers
> Rongeront de leurs cors les ôs tous descouvers,
> Et leur test, qui sera, dans un lieu solitaire,
> L'effroyable ornement d'un ombreux cimetiere:...

This argument is answered by others, analogous with Christian belief, but taken from Plutarch. However, the calm, certain beginning of the Hymn is already ruffled, the Christian dipped in pagan mythology and philosophy: a characteristic of the Hymns in general, which comes out very clearly in the next passage, with its mingling of Telephos and Christ, Achilles and God.

From line 142, Ronsard elaborates his original theme of the fleeting and ephemeral nature of life and the misery of the state of man: these lines remind us of the later developments on the same lines in Montaigne, and indeed both have a probable source in Plutarch, although a study of the original texts of the Classics is scarcely needed for some of the commonplaces involved. Remaining with the Ancients, Ronsard changes his ground again, however, and cites the opinion of Achilles delivered in hell, arguing then once more in favour of mutability and the trivial, day-to-day change-ability and death of man who is but a 'mutation qui n'a constance aucune'. Then immediately, and almost before we have time to register and digest this picture which fits in so admirably with the baroque picture of a wormful death cited above, the poet gives us a further, again contrasting, outlook on the problem, beginning with a magnificent, slow, almost nostalgic evocation of the sun's beneficence and warmth:

> ... qu'il n'est rien si beau que de voir la lumiere
> Du Soleil, qui n'est pas seulement douce & chere
> Aux hommes sains & fortz, mais aux vieux chargez d'ans,
> Perclus, estropiatz, caterreux, impotens:...

Here, if anywhere in this poem, we seem to see the non-philosophical Ronsard—the Ronsard whose reading chimes in accord with his experience and feelings. Thus we return to a fear of death and the nether regions, only leaving this fearful, pagan climate once more for a Christian peroration which yet retains striking elements of pagan mythology, together with a vision of the life according to Christ, which seems at first sight neither exact not yet exacting:

> Quiconques dis cecy, ha, pour Dieu! te souvienne
> Que ton âme n'est pas payenne, mais chrestienne,
> Et que nostre grant Maistre, en la Croix estendu
> Et mourant, de la Mort l'aiguillon a perdu,
> Et d'elle maintenant n'a faict qu'un beau passage
> A retourner au Ciel, pour nous donner courage
> De porter nostre croix, fardeau leger & doux,
> Et de mourir pour luy, comme il est mort pour nous,
> Sans craindre, comme enfans, la nacelle infernalle,
> Le rocher d'Ixion, & les eaux de Tantalle,
> Et Charon, & le chien Cerbere à trois abbois,
> Desquelz le sang de Christ t'afranchît en la Croix,
> Pourveu qu'en ton vivant tu luy veuilles complaire,
> Faisant ses mandemens qui sont aisez à faire:
> Car son joug est plaisant, gracieux & leger,
> Qui le dôs nous soulaige en lieu de le charger.

From this picture of death to the normal Renaissance picture of life in its ordinary state of flux and change is a short step. Thence we go to a striking allegorical description of Death, and after this parenthesis, full of visual appeal to the so-called medieval mind, the Hymn ends on a commonplace 'philosophical' note, reminiscent of many another poem in which Ronsard has traced out in verses musical but lacking in detail the picture of life as perpetual flux in an ocean of passing time:

Que ta puissance (ô Mort) est grande & admirable!
Rien au monde par toy ne se dit pardurable,
Mais tout ainsi que l'onde à-val des ruisseaux fuit...
Ainsi le temps se coulle, & le present faict place
Au futur importun qui les tallons luy trace:
Ce qui fut se refaict, tout coulle comme une eau,
Et rien dessous le Ciel ne se void de nouveau:
Mais la forme se change en une autre nouvelle,
Et ce changement là, VIVRE au monde s'appelle,
Et MOURIR, quand la forme en une autre s'en va.
    Ainsi, avec Venus la Nature trouva
Moyen de r'animer par longs & divers changes,
La matiere restant, tout cela que tu manges:...

The philosophical and logical indecision of the Hymn is made
even clearer by the ending, which makes an appeal to purely
immediate and human feelings, bringing in suddenly a change
which is perhaps not altogether relevant and deciding that the
author's choice is a religious or patriotic death in battle.

This Hymn, then, appears to be an exposition of various
attitudes towards death, and it is reasonable to conclude that
Ronsard has at this time no settled form of belief on the subject. This may supply a warning. Are we, as has been alleged,
in the presence of a man obsessed by various sorts of super-
stition and fear,[1] or are we not rather in the presence of a
poet, deliberately mysterious, who follows the feeling of his
age in being unable or unwilling to make up his mind between the host of alternatives offered by a creative power,
now generous and delight-giving, now dealing out sudden
change and death and always remarkable for the variety of its
gifts. The poet is a combination of dealer in eloquence and
teller of parables which are not always 'true' or explicable or

[1] As A. M. Schmidt seems inclined to suggest in the chapter on Ronsard
in his excellent study: *La Poésie scientifique en France au seizième siècle* (Paris,
1938).

needing explanation. The choice is rarely made between delightfulness and didacticism[1] and, in fact, the poet can scarcely be expected to state precisely the alternative he himself prefers: his task is more involved in mystery, more simple and yet more difficult than that, and consequently, it is frequently the reader who makes a choice which the poet has no need to make, and who gives the poem a unity which the poet would not perhaps have granted it himself.

No less significant is the picture of the sublunar universe which is indirectly conveyed in the *Hymne des Daimons*. After the dedication, the poem proper begins with a calm statement of the structure of the universe according to the poet, who sees it as being divided up into three parts: the terrestrial (comprising *Onde* and *Terre*), the aerial (inhabited by the *daimons*) and the heavenly (inhabited by the angels). He then defines more fully the area inhabited by the *daimons*:

> Plus bas qu'eux, dedans l'air dessoubz la Lune espars,
> Air gros, espaix, brouillé, qui est de toutes pars
> Tousjours remply de ventz, de fouldres & d'orages,
> Habitent les Daimons au millieu des nuages,...[2]

The limits within which these creatures must have their being are quite exactly indicated by the poet, and it is worth noting that it is in fact God who sets these and who keeps the *daimons* from transgressing them. Even so, neither the area nor indeed the make-up of the *daimons* themselves and their duties is as strictly and as 'scientifically' defined by Ronsard as might have been the case in a Peletier du Mans demonology: they remain mysterious powers, although their immediate function in Ronsardian cosmology is quite clear.

They are by no means divorced from the ordinary ex-

---

[1] Cf. an interesting passage by Pontus de Tyard: *Solitaire premier*, ed. Baridon (Geneva, 1950), p. 52.

[2] Laum., vol. VIII, p. 119.

periences of human vision. Indeed Ronsard, following
Psellos,[1] introduces the reader to them by comparing their
fantastic shapes and movements with those of the clouds (in
whose area they have their being). This comparison is
enlarged into a development which brings the reader directly
into the picture, enabling his imagination to gain a grip upon
a familiar reality before being launched into a world which
will at first seem less real:

> Ne plus ne moins qu'on voit l'exercite des nües,
> En un temps orageux egalement pendües
> D'un juste poix en l'air, marcher ainsi qu'il faut,...
> En cent diversitez, dont les vents les transforment
> En Centaures, Serpens, Oiseaux, Hommes, Poissons,
> Et d'une forme en l'autre errent en cent façons...[2]

The forms adopted by these creatures are thus immediately
intelligible, and we have no need to struggle with the abstrac-
tions of geometrical shapes, nor with any flights of extra-
human fancy. Even so, the *daimons* undoubtedly act upon the
imagination: in particular they produce the bad dreams which
are so often a feature of Ronsard's poetry. They are perhaps
in this sense allegorical figures: the concrete realization of a
not easily tangible psychological experience (usually a conflict). Ronsard's own opinions are kept well in the background,[3] but it is typical of what we see elsewhere in his
poetry that he should have chosen to illustrate the corre-
spondence between the supernatural and the human in the
world of dreams:

> Tout ainsi les Daimons font leurs masqueures voir
> A nostre fantasie, apte à les reçevoir:

---

[1] M. Psellos: a dialogue on demonology, translated into French as: *Traicté
par dialogue de l'energie des diables*, and first published in 1576.
[2] Laum., vol. VIII, p. 120. Cf. Laum., vol. V, p. 47.
[3] Cf. Laum., vol. VIII, p. 124.

Puis nostre fantasie à l'Esprit les r'apporte
De la mesme façon & de la mesme sorte
Qu'elle les imagine, ou dormant, ou veillant:
Et lors une grand'peur va noz cœurs assaillant,
Le poil nous dresse au chef, & du front goutt-à-goutte
Jusques à noz talons la sueur nous degoutte.

There follows a long development in which the *daimons*
appear as the powers behind the world of demigods and
nymphs, which inhabit the whole of fertile and living nature
—they are in fact concrete manifestations of the supernatural,
almost magic powers of Nature, of the spirit which moves
and flickers within all aspects of the created world. Even
so, however extraordinary and eccentric, even mischievous,
they may appear to be, they are subject to the control of
God and one word from their master puts them effectively in
their place. The poet's Christian orthodoxy in these matters
is emphasized by the tone of the 'personal' experience he cites
and by the invocation which concludes the poem, which is
specifically Christian in tone and sentiment.

Thus, this Hymn is an occasion for the poet to exhibit his
knowledge of a complicated, curious and erudite subject, full
of strange echoes and legends. It displays his delight in
titillating the imagination of the reader (and also of course his
own) in a type of horror story, and it may also be regarded
as an attempt at exorcism by repetition and by imitation.
Above all, however, the poem seems intended as a kind of
phantasmagoria of the sublunar universe, and a plastic repre-
sentation of the type of forces, ungoverned, uninhibited (save
should they overstep certain non-human limits, by the
superior power of a Christian God) which make this world
so fascinating and so uncertain in its accidents. Again, with
all this, the Hymn can be seen as an example of the poet's
desire to escape from the reality of existence into a more con-

vincing and more real poetic universe, into which the
imagination is introduced step by step.

In the *Hymne de la Philosophie*, Ronsard investigates, perhaps rather superficially, the possibilities and powers of
human knowledge. Here, we have a repertory of headings—
strongly evocative rather than scientifically persuasive, and
displaying the vagueness and mystery of poetry rather than
the precise knowledge of science. Philosophy appears as
difficult and austere, dwelling on 'le haut d'un Rocher', the
approach to which is by a narrow, thorny path.[1] It is worth
noting that this medieval description of the rock of Philosophy disappears in the 1584 edition. Perhaps we are to
assume that, by this time, Ronsard was more in agreement
with Montaigne:

> Elle (la sagesse) a pour son but la vertu, qui n'est pas, comme
> dit l'eschole, plantée à la teste d'un mont coupé, rabotteux et
> inaccessible. Ceux qui l'ont approché, la tiennent, au rebours,
> logée dans une belle plaine fertile et fleurissante...[2]

An admirable manifesto of the extralunar Hymns is to be
seen in the evocative, almost magical opening of the *Hymne
de l'Eternité*:

> Remply d'un feu divin qui m'a l'ame eschauffée,
> Je veux mieux que jamais, suivant les pas d'Orphée,
> Decouvrir les secretz de Nature & des Cieux,
> Recherchez d'un esprit qui n'est point ocieux:
> Je veux, s'il m'est possible, attaindre à la louange
> De celle qui jamais pour les ans ne se change,
> Mais bien qui faict changer les siecles & les temps,
> Les moys, & les saisons & les jours inconstans,
> Sans jamais se muer,...[3]

---

[1] Cf. ibid., p. 97.
[2] Montaigne, *Essais*, Book I, Chap. XXVI.   [3] Laum., vol. VIII, p. 246.

F

Once again, as the Hymn begins, Ronsard brings us immediately into the realm of the concrete, with an allegorical presentation of the protagonists of the Hymn: Eternity herself and her enemy, Discord. A host of other figures appear among whom we immediately notice a slight but remarkably effective sketch of Nature.

After this allegorical beginning, which indeed occupies the major part of the Hymn, and which is perhaps justified in the illumination of so difficult a subject, Ronsard, after passing references (still allegorical) to generation and the continuation of the species through Venus and Nature, ends the Hymn with a comparison between time and eternity, and the different types of movement implied by these two:

> Nous aultres journalliers, nous perdons la memoire
> Des temps qui sont passez, & si ne pouvons croire
> Ceux qui sont à venir, comme estans imperfaictz,...
> Mais ferme tu retiens dedans ton souvenir
> Tout ce qui est passé, & ce qui doibt venir,
> Comme haulte Deesse eternelle, & perfaicte,
> Et non ainsy que nous de masse impure faicte.

This fills and creates a pause before the final invocation of Eternity herself in terms which are neither allegorical nor medieval, but which are saturated with neoplatonism:

> Tu es toute dans toy, ta partie, & ton tout,
> Sans nul commencement, sans meillieu, ne sans bout,
> Invincible, immuable, entiere, & toute ronde,
> N'ayant partie en toy, qui dans toy ne responde,
> Toute commencement, toute fin, tout meillieu,
> Sans tenir aucun lieu, de toutes choses lieu,
> Qui fais ta deité du tout par tout estandre,
> Qu'on imagine bien, & qu'on ne peult comprendre.

It is to be noted that this Hymn is one of the very few to

make no attempt to combine the pagan and the Christian.
The poet refers to Orpheus and to Venus: otherwise the
whole of his mythology is allegorical, with a vague reference
to Gods, to the goddess Eternity, and with no references
whatsoever to Christian mythology. Apparently for once the
extralunar stands on its own, and the universe is allowed to
move in its different ways without the interference or the
control of any unique extra-universal power.

The invocation which ends the Hymn leads us naturally to
the *Hymne du Ciel,* which develops the neoplatonic tone, and
in many ways links up with the *Hymne de l'Eternité*. Here,
there is no allegorical picture, but the universe is first of all
put before us in as concrete a form as possible:

> O Ciel net, pur, & beau, haute maison de Dieu,
> Qui prestes en ton sein à toutes choses lieu,
> Et qui roules si tost ta grand'boule esbranlée
> Sur deux essieux fichez...
>
> O Ciel viste & dispos, qui parfais ton grand Tour
> D'un pied jamais recreu, en l'espace d'un jour,...[1]

Rapid and regular movement is suggested by this, and the
actual direction and force of this vitality is brought before
us in the next section of the Hymn:

> L'Esprit de l'Eternel qui avance ta course,
> Espandu dedans toy, comme une grande source
> De tous costez t'anime, & donne mouvement,
> Te faisant tournoyer en sphere rondement,
> Pour estre plus parfaict, car en la forme ronde
> Gist la perfection qui toute en soy abonde:...

In fact this poem is concerned with the movement and harmony of the heavens, their composition (which is of a 'feu

[1] Laum., vol. VIII, pp. 141–2.

vif & subtil') and their completeness and unity: the *Ciel* is seen largely as a symbol of God and his powers. All this is translated into terms of movement—an entirely different movement from the idiosyncratic, spiral, suddenly changing movement of the *Hymne des Daimons*. Ronsard succeeds in making us feel and visualize this movement of the universe 'en sphere rondement', where all is harmony and where regularity and immensity bring about stillness. The result of this is not a scientific estimate of the universe and its powers: it is a type of beauty which is expressed in a fashion peculiar to the Renaissance:

> Qui te contemplera ne trouvera sinon
> En toy qu'un ornement, & qu'une beauté pure,
> Qu'un compas bien reiglé, qu'une juste mesure,
> Et bref, qu'un rond parfaict, dont l'immense grandeur,
> Hauteur, largeur, bihays, travers, & profondeur
> Nous monstrent, en voyant un si bel edifice,
> Combien l'Esprit de Dieu est remply d'artifice,...[1]

So far we have seen the difference between sub- and extralunar worlds expressed mainly in terms of movement, to-and-fro and circular. They may also be seen in terms of light and dark. In the *Hymne des Daimons*, for example, the main scene takes place in the dark: the atmosphere is that of a dream world in which shadowy, supernatural forces have tremendous power. It is in fact only by means of light that we become aware of the extralunar world around us: whether this be the light of the stars, of the sun or of the planets—a steady light at all events, not the deceiving will o' the wisp of the *daimon*. To put it in its simplest terms:

> Mais l'homme est malheureux qui ne voit le soleil...[2]

---

[1] Laum., vol. VIII, p. 145. [2] Ibid., p. 256.

The belief in the therapeutic effect, for the soul as well as for the body, of the contemplation and the 'absorption' of light, the belief that this is particularly necessary to the poet as a step on the path towards a type of sanctity which will make unity with the One more possible, is well expressed by Ficino:

> ... l'esprit est principalement nourry de ces quatre, je dy du vin & de son odeur, & du chant & pareillement de la lumiere... Parquoy disposez vous par chascun jour à recevoir la lumiere du Soleil de sorte qu'autant que faire se pourra... n'oublians pas cependant la Lyre et le chant... souspirez d'air vivant de lumiere... prenez de vin en mesme proportion que la lumiere assez abondamment toutes fois.[1]

Generally, then, Ronsard gives us in the Hymns a picture of the universe which bears witness rather to the plastic imagination of the poet than to his scientific knowledge. Allegory in particular and also mythology are important. There are *fables* and we are faced with certain individual deities; there is description of natural *décor* and the poet often moves from a realistic and tangible basis to the fantastic, the imaginative and even the mystical. We are invited to associate ourselves with what purports to be a personal contact between the poet and a number of *daimons*, and we are asked to join him in meditation and contemplation before the shrine of an eternal being. The total impression we derive from these Hymns is not that of a *concrete* picture. The poet proceeds from the senses, but passes rapidly to an intuitive grasp of the cosmos —there is little reasoning or philosophizing, even less meteorology. The poet is voluntarily mysterious and, despite his announced wish to 'descouvrir les secretz' of Nature, we are not told in detail what these secrets are or may be. We are

[1] *Les trois livres...*, p. 180.

instead shown a vision of the extralunar world and we learn
the lesson that for mankind harmony has continually to be
reconquered, and appears as a kind of escape based on the
contemplation and absorption of worlds other than the
sublunar.[1]

The magnificent and peaceful dignity of the heavens
appears in Ronsard's poetry even in 1550:

> Et d'ordre fit dancer aus Cieus
> Le bal des estoilles coulantes.
> Elle courba le large tour
> De l'air, qui cerne tout autour
> Le rond du grand parc où nous sommes,...[2]

And although this sky (which is so often described at night,
with its accompaniment of stars, for complete darkness is
terrifying, as we see in the *Hymne des Daimons*) is an excuse
for delicate periphrasis in certain poems,[3] a starry sky is
nearly always a symbol of peace and comfort to the poet.
This appears in 1550:

> Mais quand le paresseus voile
> De la nuit quitte les cieus,
> Et que nulle & nulle estoille
> Plus ne se monstre à nos yeus,...[4]

---

[1] Jean Pierre de Mesmes, whose name appears among a list of the *Brigade*
in 1553 (Laum., vol. V, p. 179, and vol. II, p. 213), suggests in *Les institutions
astronomiques* (Paris, 1557) that a knowledge of the universe leads to inner
harmony: 'Voyla la vraye harmonie, voyla l'accord & parfaicte musique, qui
n'est autre chose que sçavoir l'ordre & sequence des choses tant celestes que
elementaires' and says that: 'je me deliberay contempler la divine harmonie
des cieux, tant pour sa constance eternelle, que perfection uniforme'.

[2] Laum., vol. III, p. 6.

[3] Cf. Laum., vol. XV, p. 70.

[4] Laum., vol. II, p. 142.

and again in 1578, just as the sky darkens in the evening:

> Telle couleur à la nuict est commune,
> D'un peu de noir sa face embellissant,
> Quand peu à peu le jour est finissant,
> Et ja le soir tire devers la brune...
> Il estoit nuict, et les humides voiles
> L'air espaissi de toutes parts avoyent,
> Quand pour baller les Dames arrivoyent,
> Qui de clairté paroissoyent des estoiles.[1]

In 1563, the peacefulness of evening consoles the poet against the 'injures et calomnies' of his enemies:

> Puis, quand la nuit brunette a rangé les estoilles,
> Encourtinant le ciel et la terre de voilles,
> Sans soucy je me couche...[2]

And the same picture is accompanied by the harmony attached to the idea of roundness (more correctly, *sphericity!*) in descriptions from 1552:

> ... sçavoir la courbe trace
> Des feux qui dancent par les Cieux.[3]

to 1569:

> Les Astres clairs, lorsqu'une nuict sereine
> D'une grand' dance en biais les pourmeine...[4]

a conception which is made more precise by the following lines from the *Hymne du Ciel*:

> Te faisant tournoyer en sphere rondement,
> Pour estre plus parfaict, car en la forme ronde
> Gist la perfection qui toute en soy abonde...[5]

---

[1] Cohen, vol. I, p. 348.
[2] Laum., vol. XI, p. 145.
[3] Laum., vol. III, p. 139.
[4] Cohen, vol. II, p. 381.
[5] Laum., vol. VIII, p. 142.

Franchet suggests that these neoplatonic ideas may well have
been developed in Ronsard by a reading of Ficino's commentary on Plato's *Ion*.[1] Despite the simplicity of Ronsard's
celestial imagery, there is a kinship with Ficino, for harmony
and science are intimately bound up in the poet's mind.
Nature herself rarely appears as a personification, for she is
rather a force of continuation and *semences* than a force of
absolute harmony.

The Hymns are in fact in many ways a picture of the
universality of creation, a plea for the universal appeal of
beauty, however naïve the poet's implied definitions of
beauty may occasionally appear. Ronsard combines strikingly,
but not always suavely, the pagan and the Christian, and in a
poem published after his death, a definition of the genre of
the Hymn, he suggests that both are in fact subordinate to
the ideal of beauty as he conceives it:

> Les Hynnes sont des Grecs invention premiere.
> Callimaque beaucoup leur donna de lumiere,
> De splendeur, d'ornement. Bons Dieux! quelle douceur,
> Quel intime plaisir sent-on autour du cœur
> Quand on lit sa Delos...
> Ah! les Chrestiens devroient les Gentils imiter
> A couvrir de beaux liz & de roses leurs testes,
> Et chommer tous les ans, à certains jours de festes,
> La memoire et les faicts de nos Saincts immortels,
> Et chanter tout le jour autour de leurs autels;...[2]

The poems published just after the Hymns—between 1556
and 1560—suggest that Ronsard was increasingly interested
in the didactic: in an elegy published in 1559[3] he seems in
fact to deny completely the usual belief of the *Pléiade* poets

[1] H. Franchet: *Le poète d'après Ronsard* (Paris, 1923), Chap. I.
[2] Cohen, vol. II, p. 652.   [3] Laum., vol. X, p. 107 ff.

that *elocution* is the mainspring of the poet's art and he appears
to think it necessary to offer his readers an increasing number
of philosophical commonplaces.[1]

The allegorical figures of Fortune and Peace[2] seem to
dominate the poems which are put together in Laumonier's
ninth volume under the title of *Opuscules de 1558–1559*.
Among these poems there are also a number of pastorals
containing the normal commonplaces about solitude, sometimes, however, dressed in relatively individual garb:

> J'estoits fasché de tant suivre les Rois,
> Et pour la Court je me perdois es bois
> Seul à part moy sauvage & solitaire,
> Loing des Seigneurs, des Rois, & du vulgaire.
> Plus me plaisoit un rocher bien pointu,
> Un antre creux, de mousse revestu,
> Un long destour d'une seule valée,
> Un vif surjon d'une onde reculée...[3]

Ronsard, then, continues to investigate and describe the
detail of Nature's creation, despite his growing interest in
other aspects,[4] which appear in a number of poems, notably
the elegy which was to be entitled in 1567: *De l'excellence de
l'esprit de l'homme.*[5] The main point of this poem is its rejec-
tion of rigidity in any form. The soul of man is compared
with the Creator and in both these manifestations of immor-
tality the main thing observed by the poet is variety within
unity:

> ... d'une plus noble essence
> Nostre esprit est formé, lequel a retenu
> Le naturel du lieu duquel il est venu.

---

[1] Cf. Laum., vol. IX, p. 112.

[2] Cf. ibid., pp. 25, 107, 112, 117, 166.   [3] Ibid., p. 174.

[4] Cf. his description of the *Grotte de Meudon* (Laum., vol. IX, p. 78). Also
Laum., vol. IX, pp. 92, 99, etc.

[5] Laum., vol. X, p. 101.

> Car tout ainsi que Dieu en variant exerce,
> Estant simple & un, sa puissance diverse,
> Et se monstre admirable en ce grand Univers
> Pour la varieté de ses effaits divers:
> Ainsi nostre ame seule, image trespetite
> De l'image de Dieu, le tout puissant imite
> D'un sutil artifice, & de sa deité
> Nous monstre les effaits par sa diversité.

The essence of the soul in fact is 'disposte & mobile': in this poem it is seen as a guiding principle, subtle, elusive but penetrating, inspiring and ordering the material envelope.

The poetry published by Ronsard in the 1560's and later seems only rarely preoccupied by 'scientific' questions. We must, however, make at least one exception. A poem in the 1569 collection—*Le Chat*—has aroused particular controversy, for its beginning has suggested to several critics that Ronsard is to be accused of pantheism and that his apparent belief in *l'âme du monde* is not consistent with strict orthodoxy. These are the lines:

> Dieu est par tout, par tout se mesle Dieu,
> Commencement, la fin, & le millieu
> De ce qui vit, & dont l'Ame est enclose
> Par tout, & tient en vigueur toute chose
> Come nostre Ame infuse dans noz corps.
>   Ja des longtemps les membres seroient morts
> De ce grand Tout, si cette Ame divine
> Ne se mesloit par toute la Machine,
> Luy donnant vie & force & mouvement:
> Car de tout estre elle est commencement.[1]

Whatever the religious orthodoxy of this passage, it is certainly highly orthodox from the point of view of Renaissance science. It is a rash critic who is prepared to distinguish abso-

[1] Laum., vol. XV, p. 39.

lutely between the various fine shades of belief, in so far as
we can use this term, which appear in works written about
this time, some of which are averroist, some neoplatonist,
some Aristotelian, some merely commonplace. H. Busson suggests[1] that this poem may well show Ronsard as an averroist,
yet the following passage from the neoplatonist Ficino
expounds ideas which are, to say the least of it, similar:

> Certainement le corps mondain autant qu'il apparoist par le
> mouvement & la generation, est par tout vivant, ce que les
> Philosophes des Indes prouvent, d'autant qu'en tous lieux il
> engendre de soy choses vivantes. Il vit donc par l'Ame qui luy
> est par tout presente, et du tout appropriee... L'esprit du monde...
> Et quant à luy c'est un corps fort tenue et delié, presque non
> corps, et presque non ame... En sa vertu il y a bien peu de nature
> terrienne, et plus d'aqueuse plus encor d'aerienne, et beaucoup
> de la nature de feu et des estoilles.... mais luy il a par tout
> vigueur, en toutes choses estant le prochain autheur et mouve-
> ment de toute generation, duquel Vergile a chanté, *L'Esprit
> nourrit par dedans tout le Monde...*
>
> ... outre ce corps de monde familierement manifeste aux sens,
> en luy est caché un certain corps spirituel, excedant la capacité
> du sens caduque et perissable... En tout endroit donques la
> nature est Magicienne, comme dit Plotin et Synesie...[2]

The borderline is fine between Nature as a force controlling
the universe and leading to harmony such as is described by
so many scientific and philosophical writers of the time and
the conception of Nature as a spirit infused into all things,
as indeed she appears in the *Hymne du Ciel*:

> L'Esprit de l'Eternel qui avance ta course,
> Espandu dedans toy, comme une grande source
> De tous costez t'anime, & donne mouvement,...[3]

---

[1] In: *Sur la philosophie de Ronsard* (*Rev. des Cours et Conférences*, 1929, pp. 32–48, 172–85).

[2] *Les trois livres...*, pp. 100, 184.   [3] Laum., vol. VIII, p. 142.

Similarly, there is interpenetration between the 'Esprit de
l'Eternel' and the soul of man and, on a lower plane, between
the soul and the body. La Primaudaye expresses this simply
enough in his *Academie françoise*:

> ... il est force que tout ainsi que tout ce qui a mouvement au
> globe universel, est maintenu par accordans discords, il y ait
> aussi entre le corps & l'ame une telle harmonie, que de l'aide de
> l'un, l'autre subsiste, & qu'avec leurs combats continuels, l'un,
> puis l'autre, soit en fin obey.[1]

As Ronsard himself puts it in rather more commonplace and
less philosophical terms in 1569:

> Le grand Platon en ses œuvres nous chante
> Que nostre Esprit comme le corps enfante
> L'un, des enfans qui surmontent la mort,
> L'autre, des filz qui doibvent voir le port
> Où le Nocher tient sa gondolle ouverte
> A tous venants, riche de nostre perte.[2]

The difficulty of resolving such an argument or defining at
all closely the terms of any discussion on this type of belief
in the sixteenth century can be judged by the distance we now
find ourselves from the original point at issue. In fact, the
idea, running through the century, of a world in continual
but controlled flux, and in which room must be found for God
and for Nature, for the authority of the Church and that of
the perhaps more frequently consulted texts of the pagan
philosophers, is bound to lead to a pantheism that is un-
acknowledged and largely involuntary. In some senses of this
inexact term, any neoplatonist may find he is a pantheist, and
it is even more apparent that, in the philosophic and scientific

---

[1] We quote from the third edition published in 1581, p. 6.
[2] Laum., vol. XV, p. 21.

writings of the century, the idea of *l'âme du monde* is a commonplace.[1]

In 1572, in the *Franciade*, Ronsard again deals with the problem of the way in which the soul is made up, and its function in the universe:

> Seigneur Troyen, tout ce qui vit au monde
> Est composé de la terre et de l'onde,
> D'air et de feu (membres de l'univers),
> Et bien qu'ils soient quatre Elemens divers
> Ils sont entre-eux liez de telle sorte
> Que l'un à l'autre enchesné se raporte,
> Et s'empruntant d'un accord se refont,
> Et changeant d'un en l'autre s'en revont.
>
> Or' tout ainsi que les hommes sans ame
> (Ame surjon de la divine flame)
> Ne pourroient vivre, ains mourroient sans avoir
> Un esprit vif qui le corps faict mouvoir,
> Et chaut et pront par les membres a place:
> Ainsi la grande universelle mace
> Verroit par mort ses membres discordans,
> S'elle n'avoit un esprit au dedans
> Infus par tout qui l'agite et remuë,
> Et dont sa course en vie est maintenuë,
> Esprit actif meslé par ce grand Tout
> Qui n'a milieu, commencement ny bout.[2]

---

[1] To return to *Le Chat*, it would appear that it was written at least partly on account of the translation by Rémy Belleau of a number of passages from Aratus (cf. Laum., vol. XV, p. 47, note). A passage from this translation (Belleau: *Œuvres poétiques*, ed. C. Marty-Laveaux, Paris, 1878, vol. II, p. 328) mentions the *suites eternelles* of the cycles of Nature. We also find that Ficino associates the name of Aratus particularly with the theme of the life of the universe: 'Je vous prie quelle folie est-ce... de ne vouloir pas que vive tout l'Univers, auquel nous vivons, nous mouvons et nous sommes? Ce qu'a chanté le Poëte Arate, signifiant Jove la commune vie du corps mondain' (*Les trois livres...*, p. 194).

[2] Laum., vol. XVI, p. 284.

Here the soul is to be seen as a *spiritus* holding together the life of the elements within us, which is a life of flux. Again our interest is gripped by the corollary of this theory: that the universe, the macrocosm, has a life which is based upon these same principles of directed flux: God is *esprit*, the elements are *corps*. We are also attracted by what appears to be a sideline: our body is described contemptuously as *souillure*, but even so, after the washing in Lethe, the spirit's first desire is to return to the world of the senses and particularly to the light of the sun.[1]

The *Hymne des Estoilles*, published in 1575,[2] shows us a universe which moves in a manner between that of the *Hymne des Daimons* and the *Hymne du Ciel*. Although the stars belong to the extralunar universe and therefore form part of the stable world, there is nevertheless considerable contact and interaction between them and man, the creature of the sublunar universe, the instability and change of whose life, according to the astrologers, is influenced by the stars, as the tides are controlled by the waxing and waning of the moon.

Ronsard is not perfectly certain of the permanence and durability of this connection and influence. The result is that the movement involved in this Hymn is much less rigid than one might have expected—there is a graceful hesitancy which appears almost as an implied expression of the elasticity of the conception of man's Free Will, acting as a sort of cushion between perception and action—the stars pull, but man does not follow them immediately or completely. So that, instead of the calm, harmonious, remorseless circular movement normally associated with the heavens, the stars are seen to move almost in a spiral. The comings and goings of the human universe remain attached to, but not absolutely controlled by the complicated mechanism, the intricate evolutions

[1] Cf. Laum., vol. XVI, p. 289.   [2] Cohen, vol. II, p. 196.

of the astronomical universe. The physical world, incapable of independent reasoning, is continually and frankly controlled by the movements of the stars. Man himself cannot escape this surge of repetitive movement and he follows the river of his Destiny. Yet this apparent compulsion is not absolute. The divine flame within us, which controls our real movements, which makes up our entelechy, is separated in some way from this physical determinism:

> Nostre esprit, une flame agile
> Qui vient de Dieu, depend de soy;
> Au corps vous donnez vostre loy,
> Comme un potier à son argile.
> ... Telle est du Ciel la loy certaine,
> Qu'il faut souffrir et non forcer:...

Thus we are in the middle, between the physical world around us, subject to the law of Nature and Destiny, and the world of the stars, moving steadily but mysteriously above us, involved in our fate but not controlling it absolutely:

> Astres, qui tout voyez,
> Ou soit que vous soyez
> Des bosses allumées,
> Ou de testes de cloux
> Ardantes de feu roux,
> Dans le Ciel enfermées,
> Je vous salue, heureuses flames,
> Estoiles, filles de la Nuit,
> Et ce Destin, qui nous conduit,
> Que vous pendistes à nos trames.
> Tandis que tous les jours
> Vous devvidez vos cours
> D'une danse etherée,
> Endurant, je vivray,
> Et la chance suivray,
> Que vous m'avez livrée.

Ronsard manages to make a compromise with the laws of a compulsive Nature, retaining a view of the universe in which man's place can be kept for him as an entity moving as it were on the end of a flexible leash: bound and not bound to the law of Nature and the decrees of Destiny. We have seen that this view is reproduced, however vaguely, in the movement of the Hymn we have just considered,[1] and this is repeatedly true of Ronsard's poetry, where three things frequently coincide: a way of writing and arranging poetry, a view of the universe and of man's place in it, and an attitude to beauty in life and in art.

The attitude of the sixteenth century towards beauty is, not unexpectedly, an ill-defined one. As late as in 1570, Lefèvre de la Boderie, in the *Encyclie*, a neoplatonist poem, describes a *beautiful* seascape as follows:

> Et quelle est la beauté de la Mer colorée,
> D'Isles, de Mons, de Rocs distinguée en meins lieus?
> Quelle est l'amenité de la rive, & orée,
> La plaisance des ports tant agreables aus yeus?
> Puis voyez comme elle est de vaisseaus decorée
> Chargés d'Or, de Joyaus, & parfuns precieus:
> Comme la Terre on void reluire en villes belles,
> La Mer on void aussi reluire en caravelles.[2]

That the sea should be valued as a spectacle because it has islands and rocks in it and ships floating upon it is an idea which scarcely recommends itself to post-Romantic notions of natural beauty—the sea itself disappears when it has to be *distinguished* by the presence of islands—but it is an idea

---

[1] For a further analysis of this hymn, see M. Raymond: *Baroque et renaissance poétique* (Paris, 1955), p. 131.

[2] *Encyclie*, p. 18.

which would be seized upon avidly by the medieval and early-Renaissance mind, and by the miniaturist in particular.

This is an early conception, whereas the attitude of the later sixteenth century towards beauty is more bound up with the perception of certain laws of proportion and harmony. Cardan, the Paduan philosopher of the early part of the century, is careful to praise Vitruvius when he gives one of the few set definitions of beauty to be found in this century:

> Qu'est-ce donc que beauté? C'est chose parfaitement cognue à la veue; & ne pouvons aimer les choses incognues: & la veue cognoit les choses qui consistent de proportion simple, double, triple, quadruple, demidouble, demitriple, comme nous avons dit de la face: la veue donc est delectee des colomnes disposees en bon ordre, ou des arbres, ou des parties de la face, quand elle cognoit incontinent l'egalité, symmetrie, et bonne proportion d'icelles... tout ce qui est bien proportionné est beau...[1]

This is an ideal, and in the aesthetic of Ronsard as it appears in his poetry there seems to be room for such an ideal. Extralunar beauty is absolute harmony to be contemplated and absorbed as an inspiration, and evoked mystically as a type of incantation hankering after escape. Ronsard speaks thus of the heavens:

> Qui te contempleras ne trouvera sinon
> En toy qu'un ornement, & qu'une beauté pure,
> Qu'un compas bien reiglé, qu'une juste mesure,
> Et bref, qu'un rond parfaict, dont l'immense grandeur,
> Hauteur, largeur, bihays, travers, & profondeur
> Nous monstrent, en voyant un si bel edifice,
> Combien l'Esprit de Dieu est remply d'artifice,

---

[1] J. Cardan: *Subtilitez* (Paris, 1556), p. 275. With this definition we should associate the standard neoplatonic conception that the beauty of the human (and especially, of course, the female) face depends upon order and measure.

> Et subtil artisan, qui te bastît de rien,
> Et t'acomplît si beau, pour nous monstrer combien
> Grande est sa Majesté, qui hautaine demande
> Pour son palais royal une maison si grande.[1]

Yet this is only one of the types of beauty offered to us by the poet. Another type corresponds to the imperfections of the sublunar universe, which it manages to reconcile. It is defined in a commentary on Plato's *Symposium* published in 1558 by Louis Le Roy, humanist, platonist and translator:

> La beauté donc est certaine concurrence de diverses choses, à l'establissement d'une tierce: qui procede de la mixtion convenable, et temperament d'icelles. La convenance resultant de ceste commixtion proportionnée s'appelle beauté. Tel temperament est cause que les natures auparavant diverses et differentes conviennent et accordent ensemble à composer une autre nature, devenant la contrarieté unité, et la discorde concorde: tellement que pouvons dire ceste beauté n'estre autre chose qu'inimitié amye, et une discorde concordante. Parquoy Heraclite disoit la guerre et concorde estre pere et mere des choses...[2]

This dichotomy between absolute harmony and the proportion produced through equilibrium is paralleled in the world of poetic theory by that between the divine poet and the poet of a subsequent generation who must create, not by the pure force of inspiration, but by learning and waiting upon an inconstant poetic fury.

[1] Laum., vol. VIII, p. 145.

[2] *Sympose*, f. 108. This passage undoubtedly derives from G. Pico della Mirandola, a work translated into French and published (Paris, 1598) as: *Commentaire sur une Chanson d'amour... par H. Benivieni.* Cf. also le Roy's *Phédon* (Paris, 1553), f. 70, and his *Vicissitude* (Paris, 1578), f. 5: 'Ce n'est donc sans cause, que nature appete tant les contraires, faisant d'eux toute decense & beauté, non de semblables.' Cf. my article: 'Contraries in sixteenth century scientific writing in France' in: *Essays presented to C. M. Girdlestone* (Durham, 1960).

CHAPTER IV

Nature as Inclination and Temperament

THE preceding chapters suggest in the career of Ronsard a certain development in the direction of order.[1] The poet brings to perfection the order of classical composition in poems such as 'Quand je suis...', and from 1550 to 1556 he seems to concentrate quite deliberately upon this problem of order, once he has got out of his system the fire and fury associated with the so-called pindaric odes. But this does not appear merely in the style of his poetry. From about 1553 Ronsard turns his attention from the description of the various details of natural phenomena to a consideration of the universe as a whole and especially of the controlling power of Nature, the goddess, the âme du monde. That this consideration is poetic and even mystical rather than scientific only increases the coherence and unity of the picture presented.[2]

Cf. Laum., vol. XI, p. 167:

> Je vy que des François le langage trop bas
> Se trainoit sans vertu, sans ordre, ny compas:
> Je fis d'autre façon que n'avoient les antiques,
> Vocables composés, & frases poëtiques,
> Et mis la Poësie en tel ordre qu'apres
> Le François fut egal aux Romains & aux Grecs.

[2] Once he has attained success in these fields, he seems to lose interest—this process is continually a part of his poetic development. Thus, from the late 1550's onwards, Ronsard begins to favour more strongly the longer poem, less infected by poetic fury, and here he does not in general use this so-called classical order of presentation.

I would advance with considerable hesitation the theory that Ronsard was at least somewhat influenced in the order or *disposition* of his poetry at this time by the *Dialectique* of Pierre de la Ramée.[1] The manifestation of this influence is a very tenuous one. It is based upon a comparison of the type of *disposition* used by Ronsard after about 1555 and the following precepts by Ramus, who advocates particularly for the literary writer a method which he calls the method of prudence:

> Methode est de nature ou de prudence... S'ensuyt la methode de prudence, en laquelle les choses precedentes non pas du tout & absolument plus notoires, mais neantmoins plus convenables à celluy qui fault enseigner, & plus probables à l'induire... ou nous pretendons... Elle gist grandement en la prudence de l'homme, plus qu'en l'art & preceptes de doctrine:... Commencer au milieu, & ne poinct declarer au commencement son entreprise, ny deduire les parties d'icelle: Chercher de bien loing les moyens & antecedentz de nostre attente: & ce principalement par similitude & parabole: Et les poursuyvre incontinent, si nostre partie est imprudente: car telz espritz se laissent incontinent surprendre. Si c'est homme cault & fin, il ne fault pas incontinent manifester noz pieces l'une apres l'aultre, mais changer, entremesler frivoles: feindre le contraire... se haster, courroucer, debatre: proceder par grande hardiesse... Le poëte avecques ce qu'il est souvent en toutes parties de Logique excellent, encore est il plus en cette partie admirable: Il se propose d'enseigner le peuple, c'est à dire beste de plusieurs testes:[2] & partant deçoit par maintes manieres: Il commence au milieu & là souvent comprend le premier: finablement il conclud le dernier par quelque cas incertain & inopiné: et comme dict Horace en son art poetique:

---

[1] Ronsard contributed some translations to this work (published in 1555). For his relations with Ramus, cf. Laum., vol. X, p. 380, note.

[2] Cf. Laum., vol. VII, p. 116.

> Et tellement ses fictions pallie,
> Ainsi le vray avec le faulx il lie
> Que le milieu du premier ne differe,
> Et que la fin au milieu se refere...[1]

Thus the *disposition* of the poet depends intimately, not upon a grasp of the rules of logic and orthodox classical composition, but rather upon the imagination of the poet who is to take the reader through a poetic maze which he has arranged, for the sake of persuasion, teaching and perhaps also the demonstration of beauty, in a fashion which is bound to depend upon his own temperament and perhaps upon what he can divine of that of his reader.

This leads us back the more forcibly to the subject of nature. For, in the poems which he publishes about 1560 and thereafter, Ronsard repeatedly uses the word *nature* in the sense of temperament. He seems, in fact, to have adopted a kind of determinist attitude towards the universe, one which is not uncommon during the sixteenth century and which holds men to have various tasks and professions, imposed upon them by Fate and Fortune or by their *nature*. If we go back to the definition of Nature by Lemnius, quoted at the beginning of our second chapter, we find that he includes as a part of his definition:

> Nature est l'instinct et inclination d'un chascun.

What then is the *nature* of Ronsard, as it is disclosed in his poetry? Here we find immediately a whole theory of the nature of the poet, a curious theory, although a commonplace of the century, based mainly upon the kind of argument used by Ficino in his treatise *Les trois livres de la vie...* and repeated by other commentators. These ideas are fundamental to the

---

[1] *Dialectique*, pp. 120, 128–30.

Renaissance ideal of the man of letters, and it is curious to see that this ideal has in fact changed very little since then.

Ronsard's excursions into the world of self-analysis and introspection are rare. Indeed, before 1560 there is no sign of them, if we except an autobiographical passage addressed to Paschal, the purpose of which was purely utilitarian. Even after 1560, although self-description occurs often enough, the picture of Ronsard and his *nature* which emerges is stylized and idealized. Reality is rarely the main concern of the poet, especially of a poet who deals in the world of imagination, invention and mythology, and who bases much of his poetry on the idea of *imitation*.

Ficino's well-known picture of the ideal of the *studieux* may or may not have been a source of some of Ronsard's ideas on poetry and its composition. Certainly, however, it represents a type of the Renaissance ideal of the poet which must have been familiar to Ronsard and to his contemporaries and as such is worth reproducing.[1] The treatise is mainly medical and astrological. Even the casual, if important advice contained in it, such as the avoidance of an excess of meat and wine, revolves around the central notion that the *studieux* is subject to melancholy.[2] This fact appears clearly at the beginning of the treatise, and various reasons celestial, natural and human are adduced:

... la contemplation à son tour... attire & acquiert un naturel fort

---

[1] We quote from the translation made by Lefèvre de la Boderie and published in 1581.

[2] This idea is, of course, by no means original to Ficino. During the Renaissance it is generally attributed to Aristotle (*Problems*, 30). It should be noted that writers of the period are not unanimous in subscribing to the doctrine. Cf. J. Tahureau (*Dialogues*, Paris, 1565). I quote from p. 95 of the reprinted ed. (Paris, 1870): 'lesquels... contre tout leur naturel affectent le plus qu'ils peuvent la melancolie, pour autant qu'ils out leu en quelque passage d'Aristote que volontiers les melancoliques sont ingenieus.'

resemblant à la melancholie... au jugement des Philosophes
naturels ceste fureur mesme [fureur poétique] n'est point incitee
en d'autres qu'aux melancholiques... Car pendant que ceste
humeur s'embrase & ard, elle a de coustume de faire les hommes
émuz & furieux... Mais quand elle s'estaint estant ja les plus
subtiles & plus claires parties dissoutes & ne restant seulement
que la noire suye, elle les rend stupides & hebetez. Laquelle
habitude, on nomme... melancholie, démence & folie.[1]

This is particularly true in the old age of the poet and, in
order to avoid or mitigate this periodic engendering of dark
humours, he is advised to seek solitude:

Saturne,... a concedé à Jupiter la vie commune, & s'est
reservée la vie separée et divine. Et est en quelque sorte amy &
favorable aux entendemens des hommes qui vrayment se tiennent
delà separez & eslongnez...

and to cultivate *subtlety* and lightness. He is particularly
urged to follow his *naturel*:

Affin que viviez & ouvriez heureusement sur tout connoissez
vostre naturel, vostre Astre, & vostre Genie, & le lieu à eux
convenable habitez y, & suivez vostre profession naturelle.[1]

No way of life, however, can bring total peace to the melancholic. In fact, for Ficino, Pontus de Tyard[2] and others, the
poet alternates between prolonged and tenacious seeking after
knowledge and truth, between times when he is gripped by
fury and inspiration, and periods when he is afflicted by
melancholy, misery and spleen:

Saturne ne signifie pas facilement la commune qualité &

---

[1] Our quotations come from pp. 5, 7, 180, 171, 175 of the treatise.

[2] Cf. Pontus de Tyard: *Solitaire premier*, especially pp. 8–9 (ed. Baridon,
Geneva, 1950). It should be noted that, in several works of the century, fury
and melancholy are treated not only as platonic madnesses but actually as a
disease: cf. the pseudo-psychological work translated by G. Chappuys: *Le
Theatre des divers cerveaux du monde* (Paris, 1586), *Discours* 48.

condition du genre humain, mais l'homme separé des autres, divin,
& bien-heureux, ou pressé d'une misere brutale ou extreme.[1]

The activities, poetic and otherwise, of Ronsard in 1560
and the years following suggest that he is aware of the
dangers attaching to the profession of poet, that he realizes
that the poet, by definition, leads his life now in the heights,
now in the depths—now subject to the furious inspiration of
creation, now subject to spleen and melancholy. In the elegies
of 1560–1, the poet repeatedly puts before us the 'saturnine'
self-portrait:

> Je suis tout aggravé de somne & de paresse,
> Inhabile, inutile: & qui pis, je ne puis
> Arracher cest humeur dont esclave je suis.
>   Je suis opiniastre, indiscret, fantastique,
> Farouche, soupçonneux, triste & melancolicque,
> Content & non content, mal propre, & mal courtois:
> Au reste craignant Dieu, les princes & les lois,
> Né d'assez bon esprit, de nature assez bonne,
> Qui pour rien ne voudroit avoir faché personne:
> Voylà mon naturel, mon Grevin, & je croy
> Que tous ceux de mon art ont tels vices que moy.[2]

He laments the slowing-down consequent upon the coming
of old age, and demands fresh stimulus for his work, which
he cannot lay aside because of the forces of his Destiny, his
star, his *daimon*. Solitude and the saturnine are associated in
his mind:

> L'autre jour que j'estois, comme toujours je suis,
> Solitaire & pensif (car forcer je ne puis

---

[1] *Les trois livres...*, p. 97.
[2] Laum., vol. XIV, p. 195 (Appendix, p. 143). For other self-portraits of
Ronsard cf. Laum., vol. I, p. 213; vol. VI, p. 228; vol. VII, pp. 102, 307;
vol. VIII, p. 345; vol. X, p. 300; vol. XI, pp. 132, 150; vol. XII, p. 174.

> Mon Saturne ennemy), si loing je me promeine
> Que seul je m'esgaray de sur les bords de Seine,
> Un peu de soubs le Louvre, où les Bons-hommes sont
> Enclos estroittement de la rive & du mont.

This self-analysis, or this discovery within himself of a poetic temperament which coincides with the contemporary picture, seems to be accompanied by (or perhaps even stems from) a consciousness of criticism from outside and a need to defend himself against this criticism. Certainly this need seems to declare itself quite suddenly, and it is in 1560–1 particularly that the poet reveals so much of himself and his own ideas and ideals in a series of poems entitled 'elegies', perhaps better called 'epistles': their main interest for us, certainly, is in their autobiographical and introspective note.

In the *Elegie à Pierre l'Escot* Ronsard suggests that l'Escot, like himself, has followed his *nature* and thereby attained the success attendant upon happiness. He also makes it clear that the *nature aux muses inclinée* is closely allied to the force of youth, of imagination and of Nature:

> Je n'avois pas douze ans qu'au profond des vallées,
> Dans les hautes forets des hommes reculées,
> Dans les antres segrets de frayeur tout couverts,
> Sans avoir soing de rien, je composois des vers:
> Echo me respondoit, & les simples dryades,
> Faunes, satyres, pans, napées, oréades,
> Aigypans qui portoient des cornes sur le front,
> Et qui ballant sautoient comme les chevres font,
> Et les nimphes suivant les fantastiques fées,
> Autour de moy dançoient à cottes agrafées.[1]

The self-portraits which the poet puts before us in these elegies and in other poems published about this time are by no means always pleasant. We are aware of considerable defiance,

[1] Laum., vol. X, p. 304.

and with this goes a bitter consciousness of old age and
poverty: the requests for money are straightforward and by
no means so supple and good-humoured as those of Clément
Marot. Ronsard is old and melancholy:

> Pour elles [les Muses] à trente ans j'avoys le chef grison,
> Megre, palle, deffaict, enclos en la prison
> D'une melencolicque & reumaticque estude,
> Renfrogné, mal-courtois, sombre, pensif, & rude:
> A fin qu'en me tuant je peusse recevoir
> Quelque peu de renom par un peu de sçavoir,[1]

although this insistence upon his advanced age (he can in fact
scarcely be thirty-five) is perhaps due to an exaggerated
awareness that poetry is the profession of youth, especially
if the poet wishes to be visited by *fureur*. This idea is com-
bined with others in a striking image in this elegy to the
Seigneur l'Huillier:

> Comme on void en septembre, ez tonneaux Angevins,
> Bouillir en escumant la jeunesse des vins,
> Laquelle en son berceau à toute force gronde,
> Et vouldroit tout d'un coup sortir hors de sa bonde,
> Ardente, impatiente, & n'a point de repos
> De s'enfler, d'escumer, de jaillir à gros flotz,...
> Ainsi la poësie en la jeune saison
> Bouillonne dans noz cœurs, peu subjecte à raison,
> Serve de l'appetit, qui hautement anime
> D'un poëte gaillard la fureur magnanime:...[2]

---

[1] Laum., vol. X, p. 300. Pallor and white hair are, of course, traditional signs
of melancholy. It is worth noting that the idea of a close association between
melancholy and imagination had been in Ronsard's mind at least since 1555
(cf. Laum., vol. VII, p. 280):

> Voila comment pour estre fantastique
> En cent façons ses beaultez j'apperçoy,
> Et m'esjouys d'estre melancolique
> Pour recevoir tant de formes en moy.

[2] Ibid., p. 293.

Even so, there is as yet no suggestion of retirement. The poet must continue to follow his *nature* and others must abide his *humeur*; he must continue as he began[1] and, despite his description of one of these elegies as a 'mal plaisant escrit',[2] Ronsard is decidedly unrepentant:

> Je ne contraincts personne à mon vers poeticque,
> Le lise qui voudra, l'achette qui voudra:...
> Je suis ce que je suis, ma conscience est bonne,...[3]

and in the elegy to Grévin,[4] in a judicious and elaborate metaphor, Ronsard sums up his impression of poetic fury as it is given to mortals, resulting as it does in: 'cest humeur dont esclave je suis'.

> Le don de Poësie est semblable à ce feu,
> Lequel aux nuicts d'hyver comme un presage est veu
> Ores dessus un fleuve, ores sur une prée,
> Ores dessus le chef d'une forest sacrée,
> Sautant & jallissant, jettant de toutes pars
> Par l'obscur de la nuict de grans rayons espars.

There seem indeed to be obvious differences between the picture of poetic fury as it is given by Ronsard in 1560–1 and that given in the *Ode à Michel de l'Hospital*, published in 1552,[5] but here again we must remember the historical division of poets into generations, a division upon which Ronsard insists in this ode and elsewhere. Only in the first of these generations do we have the divine poets, those who are perfect, who do all by inspiration and in whom *nature* is not subject to art. In the 1560–1 elegies and especially in the elegy to Grévin this ideal state of things no longer persists. The practice of poetry is more up and down: indeed poetic fury

[1] Cf. ibid., p. 335.   [2] Ibid., p. 296.   [3] Ibid., pp. 363–4.
[4] Laum., vol. XIV, p. 193 (Appendix, p. 143).
[5] Cf. Laum., vol. III, pp. 144, 149.

is, significantly, presented as a will o' the wisp. Ronsard considers himself cut off from the full, eternal spring of poetic fury by at least two things: first, that he is not of the divine generation, despite his aspirations; second, that he is no longer young and effervescent. Even so, he cannot abdicate his *nature*, and the practice of poetry continues to be compulsive.

The *Discours*, published in 1562–3, are more official than these intimate elegy-epistles. But, although Ronsard is writing official Catholic poetry—or perhaps because of this fact—he himself is not completely involved in any one set of opinions. We may well assume that we are before a believing, perhaps rather an accepting Catholic Christian, for whom the truth is so simple and self-evident that it scarcely needs development or even repetition or statement, but even so, and despite the fervour of certain orthodox arguments, we are startled by passages such as the following:

> Certes si je n'avois une certaine foy...
> ... comme les premiers je deviendrois Payen.
> La nuit j'adorerois les rayons de la Lune,
> Au Matin le Soleil, la lumiere commune,
> L'œil du monde, & si Dieu au chef porte des yeux,
> Les rayons du Soleil sont ses yeux radieux,
> Qui donnent vie à tous, nous maintiennent & gardent,
> Et les faicts des humains en ce monde regardent.
> Je dy ce grand Soleil qui nous fait les saisons
> Selon qu'il entre ou sort de ses douze maisons,...
> L'esprit, l'ame du monde, ardent & flamboyant,
> En la course d'un jour tout le ciel tournoyant,
> Plain d'immence grandeur, rond, vagabond, & ferme,
> Lequel tient dessoubs luy tout le monde pour terme,
> En repos, sans repos, oisif, & sans sejour,
> Fils aysné de Nature, & le pere du jour.[1]

---

[1] Laum., vol. XI, p. 66.

Here, obviously, as in the invocation of Ceres which follows, the image has more appeal for the poet than its doctrinal pretext. Expression and belief are in a constant process of interaction and, as he says in the 1587 preface to the *Franciade*, the poet invents his own arguments: 'se servant de l'opinion de toutes sectes, selon que son argument le demande'.[1] Again, defending himself in the *Responce aux injures et calomnies*...:

> Ainsi tu penses vrais les vers dont je me joüe.[2]

Even so, we are forced to take into consideration the picture which the poet gives of himself in the *Responce*. It is undoubtedly the result of considerable thought and introspection, and is perhaps of more value than the tossing around of abstract accusations. Ronsard recognizes that upon self-knowledge depends wisdom:

> Le vray commencement pour en vertus acroistre
> C'est (disoit Apollon) soymesme se cognoistre.[3]

In fact a number of lines in the *Responce* contain the most obviously conscious and deliberate, almost Montaignian description of the poet's own everyday way of life. Certain simple, open statements make the sincerity of this confession clear enough.[4] The poet sings badly, he likes women and love and dancing. On the other hand he prays regularly and he profits from the respectability and virtue attached traditionally to the country life and to the sober, Horatian way of living. How much importance we attach to these passages must be a matter of opinion. The daily routine advocated is curiously close to that advanced by Ficino in his admonitions to the studious man, and it may well be that Ronsard is

---

[1] Laum., vol. XVI, p. 336. Cf. also a long passage on *opinion* in one of the *Discours* (Laum., vol. XI, p. 77).

[2] Laum., vol. XI, p. 163. [3] Ibid., p. 8.

[4] Cf. ibid., pp. 145, 147.

merely representing a certain conventional way of life. Certainly the serene and celebrated passage in which the poet
most fully describes his daily routine[1] is scarcely typical of a
series of poems whose rugged and forceful style and deliberate
lack of order in the conventional sense is explained in this
passage:

> Tu te moques aussi dequoy ma poësie
> Ne suit l'art miserable, ains va par fantaisie,
> Et dequoy ma fureur sans ordre se suivant,
> Esparpille ses vers comme fueilles au vent:...
>   En l'art de Poësie, un art il ne faut pas
> Tel qu'ont les Predicans, qui suivent pas à pas
> Leur sermon sceu par cueur, ou tel qu'il faut en prose,
> Où toujours l'Orateur suit le fil d'une chose.
>   Les Poëtes gaillards ont artifice à part,
> Ils ont un art caché qui ne semble pas art
> Aux versificateurs, d'autant qu'il se promeine
> D'une libre contrainte, où la Muse le meine.
> Ainsi que les Ardens aparoissant de nuit
> Sautent à divers bons, icy leur flame luit,
> Et tantost reluit là, ores sur un rivage,
> Ores desur un mont, ou sur un bois sauvage.[2]

In these poems, published between 1560 and 1563, we are
aware of a note of disillusion and defiance. Ronsard is very
conscious of the enemies, poetical and political, who surround
him. Hence, perhaps, the declarations of the preface to the
Nouveau Recueil[3] published in 1563, in which the poet replies
to actual or anticipated criticisms, poetical and personal. In

[1] Cf. Laum., vol. XI, p. 144.
[2] Ibid., pp. 159–60. For an analysis of these *Discours* see H. Weber: *La
Création poétique au XVIe. siècle en France* (Paris, 1956), pp. 559–600. It is
worth noting that, in the *Discours*, Ronsard uses at least four times the word
brusque of his poetry or his own temperament (Laum., vol. XI, pp. 123, 160,
162, 167).
[3] *Les trois livres du recueil des nouvelles poesies.*

the main he adopts the attitude of many of his contemporaries (including Du Bellay) that poetry is a light-hearted
business and that he himself is an amateur and a gentlemanly
nonchallant.[1] He lays particular emphasis upon freedom and
fantasy:

> La poësie est plaine de toute honneste liberté, & s'il faut dire
> vray un folastre mestier duquel on ne peut retirer beaucoup
> d'avancement, ny de profit. Si tu veux sçavoir pourquoy j'y
> travaille si allegrement, pource qu'un tel passetemps m'est aggre-
> able, & si mon esprit en escrivant ne se contentoit, je n'en ferois
> jamais un vers...[2]

and the fears and dreads of the melancholic Ronsard of the
early 1560's seem in abeyance. His two mentions of melancholy are both pejorative and the poet suggests particularly
that he welcomes his own return in this collection of poems
to his *naturel*, which he mentions four times in these dozen
pages. This *naturel* is humble and light-hearted. The *Discours*
are said to have been 'contre la modestie de mon naturel'.
Court poetry is said to be acceptable, provided that 'je ne
force mon naturel', and the poet declares himself to be *content*
and *resolu*, 'soit que mon naturel me rende tel, ou soit que
mon mestier le veille ainsi'; he is to follow the gentle prompt-
ings of this nature: 'Ainsi suivant mon naturel, en ceste douce
saison de la paix.' Thus, the real core of the preface lies in
the poet's desire for and adulation of freedom and liberty:

> Seulement quand il fait beau temps je me pourmeine, quand il
> pleut je me retire au logis, je devise, je passe le temps sans
> discourir, practicquer ni affecter choses plus hautes que ma
> vacation. Et voulez vous que je vous die ce qui m'a le plus
> ennuyé durant ces troubles, c'est que je n'ay peu jouyr de la
> franchise de mon esprit, ny librement estudier comme au para-
> vant. Je me plains de petite chose, ce direz vous, ouy petite

---

[1] The notion was popularized by Castiglione.   [2] Laum., vol. XII, p. 8.

> quant à vous qui avez tousjours despendu de la volonté d'autruy:
> mais grande quant à moy qui suis nourry en toute heureuse &
> honneste liberté. Aussi suivant mon naturel en ceste douce
> saison de la paix vous ne me pourriez engarder de me resjouir
> & d'escrire...[1]

It would seem that the act of creating poetry and even the studying of books imply a loosening of the bondage of life: poetry is the main step to freedom from the earthly, the bodily and perhaps also the topical and incidental.

The most important poem in this new collection from our point of view is the *Hymne de l'Automne*.[2] The eighty-six lines at the beginning form a sort of preface: a declaration of certain experiences and convictions which are personal to the poet and which are all related, implicitly, to nature: either the *inclination* of the poet, or the world which surrounds him and which he transforms into poetry. Having assured us of those truths about poetry which appear so often in the Renaissance and which we need scarcely repeat, Ronsard goes on to tell us of his youth in the country. Yet this passage is not as joyful as might have been expected, nor yet as naïve. Instead of the expected: 'Quand j'avois verts les genous...', it is the *horror* of Nature which is brought to the fore:

> Je n'avois pas quinze ans que les mons & les boys,
> Et les eaux me plaisoient plus que la court des Roys,
> Et les noires forests espesses de ramées,
> Et du bec des oyseaux les roches entamées:

---

[1] Laum., vol. XII, p. 15. On the word *liberté* in the sixteenth century, cf. the *Theatre des divers cerveaux* (Gazzoni, transl. G. Chappuys, Paris, 1586), *Discours* 31: 'Les cerveaux libres sont ceux là proprement, lesquels ont en eux, une certaine liberté de parler pour le vray... (l'homme libre) jouit de soy seul, estimant les autres, pource qu'ils sont, & se laissant estimer soy-mesme, pour celuy que les autres veulent.' This *liberté* belongs in fact only to the serious and the upright, not merely to the fantastical.

[2] Laum., vol. XII, p. 46 (Appendix, p. 148).

Une valée, un antre en horreur obscurcy,
Un desert effroiable, estoit tout mon soucy,
A fin de voir au soir les Nymphes & les Fées
Danser desoubs la Lune en cotte par les prées,
Fantastique d'esprit,...

and indeed this apparently autobiographical statement is couched in what are at first sight most unrealistic terms, belonging rather to the ritual of the ideal poetic career, even though they are attached to reality by certain details of Ronsard's childhood surroundings. Once again the poetic reality is more important than the observed facts. Description is merged into poetic emotion, and the aesthetic and emotional value of the scene are dominant.

The fate of the poet is described in a disillusioned fashion:

Tu seras du vulgaire appellé frenetique...

and once again he is advised to disguise truth under the cloak of the fable. Fables do indeed have a purpose in the work of the poet (this Hymn is centred upon a fable), but the story itself rapidly becomes more interesting than its purpose. As in the *Roman de la Rose* we become more interested in the mechanism of the allegories than in the psychological conflicts which they embody, so here we are diverted from the possible moral end of the fable to interest in the fable itself. The story is simple enough. Autumn is advised by her nurse to go and look up her parents. She is carried there by the wind *Auton*. She sees the palaces of Spring, of Summer and of Nature, she meets Bacchus, who courts her successfully, and rather hastily, the Hymn ends with the usual peroration. What is valuable is the incidental—especially the various descriptive *hors d'œuvre* which are handled with a delightful and light-hearted negligence seeming to bear out the ideals of liberty and fantasy proposed by the poet in his preface. The result

H

may be exasperating to one who insists upon unity and harmony of structure. Yet the tone and the décor of the poem
are unified: light, careless and situated in a world of the
imagination which is gently but credibly attached to the real
by means of the comparison. Here we see the spider:

> Ainsi qu'en nos jardins on voit embesongnée
> Des la pointe du jour la ventreuse Arignée,
> Qui quinze ou vingt fillets, comme pour fondement
> De sa trame future atache proprement,
> Puis tournant à l'entour d'une adresse subtile
> Tantost haut tantost bas des jambes elle file,
> Et fait de l'un à l'autre un ouvrage gentil,
> De travers, de biés, noudant tousjours le fil,
> Puis se plante au millieu de sa toille tendue
> Pour attraper le ver ou la mouche attendue.

with the curiously similar picture of the nurse spinning. There
are a number of short descriptions, such as the few words
devoted to the ploughman with his 'deux mains empoulées'
and a two-line evocation of the falcon with folded wings.
Perhaps the most realistic description is that of the threshers,
remarkable for brevity, movement and technicality. Then
there is the fine *baroque* description of the cavern of the wind
Auton. The delicacy of the mythological background is well
illustrated by the following periphrasis which indicates merely
the time of day:

> C'estoit au mesme poinct que l'estoille du jour
> Avoit desja chassé les astres d'alentour
> Des pastures du Ciel, et les contant par nombre,
> Pour la crainte du chaut les alloit mettre à l'ombre.
> Ja la Lune argentée alloit voir son amy,
> Son bel Endymion sur le mont endormy
> Et ja la belle Aurore au visage de roses
> Les barrieres du ciel par tout avoit descloses:

Et desja le Soleil son front avoit huilé
De fard, à celle fin qu'il ne fust point haslé,
Et assis dans son char desja tenoit la bride
A ses coursiers tirés hors de l'estable vuide,...

It is typical in so lively a poem that Nature should appear
above all as the force of generation. In her palace 'sont dedans
des pots... encloses... les semences des choses... Affin qu'en
vieillisant le Monde rajeunisse,...'

In the *Abbregé de l'art poëtique françois*, published in
1565,[1] Ronsard crystallizes and expresses perhaps none too
coherently some of the beliefs about poetry which have been
implicit in his work up to that date.

He makes the conventional distinction between *invention*,
disposition and *elocution*, but his definition of *invention* is
important and much more interesting than, for example, the
one which Du Bellay inserted in 1549 in the *Deffence et
Illustration*.[2] For Ronsard, invention is *le principal poinct* and
la mere de toutes choses. His definition is close to that of
Peletier du Mans,[3] who considers *invention* to have a part to
play throughout the various stages of poetic composition.
Ronsard involves *invention* with the *nature* of the poet:

Tu auras en premier lieu les conceptions hautes, grandes,
belles, & non trainantes à terre. Car le principal poinct est
l'invention, laquelle vient tant de la bonne nature, que par la
leçon des bons & anciens autheurs.

and, in a long passage, he connects it with the work of the

[1] Laum., vol. XIV, pp. 3 e.s.
[2] *Deffence*, p. 33: 'cete copie et richesse d'invention, premiere et principale
piece du harnoys de l'orateur.'
[3] *Art poétique*, p. 88: 'Ele èt repandue par tout le Poème, comme le sang
par le cors de l'animal: de sorte qu'ele se peut apeler la vie ou l'ame du Poème.'

imagination, conjuring up in the poet's mind images and forms:

> L'invention n'est autre chose que le bon naturel d'une imagination concevant les Idées & formes de toutes choses qui se peuvent imaginer tant celestes que terrestres, animées ou inanimes, pour apres les representer, descrire & imiter; car tout ainsi que le but de l'orateur est de persuader, ainsi celuy du Poëte est d'imiter, inventer & representer les choses qui sont, qui peuvent estre, ou que les anciens ont estimé comme veritables: & ne fault point douter, qu'apres avoir bien & hautement inventé, que la belle disposition des vers ne s'ensuyve, d'autant que la disposition suit l'invention mere de toutes choses, comme l'ombre faict le corps. Quand je te dy que tu inventes choses belles & grandes, je n'entends toutesfois ces inventions fantasticques & melencolicques, qui ne se rapportent non plus l'une à l'autre que les songes entrecoupez d'un frenetique... à l'imagination duquel, pour estre blessée, se representent mille formes monstrueuses sans ordre ny liayson...

It is in keeping with the cautious, Horatian note of these last lines that Ronsard should also have thought fit in this *Abbregé* to lay emphasis upon the pictorial effect and the sense of the images which are the life of poetry. Not only are the comparisons to be drawn from life, the poet stresses the appositeness and liveliness of the adjectives and expressions to be used:

> choisir... les mots plus significatifs des dialectes de nostre France, ... Je te veux advertir de fuir les epithetes naturelz,... tes epithetes seront recherchez pour signifier...

In fact the poet is to seek both the *beau* and the *significatif*. Each brick is to be considered as closely as the general architectonic effect of the poem. The true poet, as distinct from the mere versifier, is to pay attention to the fable and fiction

rather than merely to the lines he is writing, and it is implied
that he will seek out richness, avoiding the bareness of prose.
In fact the central notion of this art of poetry is summed up
in one metaphorical passage in the middle:

> car tout ainsi qu'on ne peult veritablement dire un corps humain
> beau, plaisant & accomply s'il n'est composé de sang, venes,
> arteres & tendons, & surtout d'une plaisante couleur: ainsi
> la poësie ne peut estre plaisante ny parfaicte sans belles inven-
> tions, descriptions, comparaisons, qui sont les ners & la vie du
> livre qui veult forcer les siecles pour demourer de toute memoire
> victorieux & maistre du temps.

This body must be pulsating with life, yet its life must not
get out of hand: we must rely on a *bon naturel*, and Ronsard
is firmly against exaggerated fantasies. He insists elsewhere on
this comparison of poetry with a healthy body: it is an image
which admirably describes his mature poetry.

One, furthermore, which stresses the constant parallelism
felt by Renaissance writers between the creations of the poet
and those of God and Nature. Description and imagery in the
poem correspond to the artistic creations of Nature in the
universe, for poetry is as highly wrought as the world itself.
Nature is Artist and Artist is Nature, and: 'l'invention despend
d'une gentille nature d'esprit'.

The *Sixiesme & Septiesme livres des Poëmes*, published in
1569, tell us a number of things about the intimate life of
Ronsard the countryman, and the connection, which is both
biographical and temperamental, between the poet and the
country at this time. In this way they bring us back, if not
to poems describing the *Vendômois*, such as we were dealing
with in our first chapter, at any rate to a type of nature poetry
which can be called rustic and which is concerned with the

countryside and its pleasures. Internal evidence tells us that many of these poems were written while Ronsard was kept at Saint-Côme by illness, suffering, as he says, from a *fiebvre quarte*,[1] and a number of passages contain reminiscences of Saint-Côme and Croixval, two of the benefices acquired by the poet towards the end of his life.

This collection of poems as a whole takes us very far from the high-sounding declamations of the *Deffence et Illustration*,[2] and the lighter note is emphasized by one of the very few direct imitations of Clément Marot to be found in Ronsard's poetry:

> A Mon-faucon tout sec puisses-tu pendre,
> Les yeux mangez de corbeaux charongneux,
> Les pieds tirez de ces mastins hargneux,
> Qui vont grondant herissez de furie,...[3]

Laumonier has described Ronsard as 'un Marot supérieur'. Certainly the amusing is often present in this collection[4] and there are continually simple pastoral touches in the *Salade* and the *Hylas*. But, in this last instance, the details of building a fire and cooking a supper, pastoral and natural as they are, can be seen as homeric at least as much as neo-marotic.[5] Similarly the moving lines in which Ronsard represents poetry as a consolation in the face of illness and old age are too grave in tone to belong to Marot, whose poetry consoles him immediately against more material misfortunes.[6]

In 1569 Ronsard is still preoccupied with the theory of

[1] M. Ficino (*Les trois livres...*, p. 8) suggests this is a disease particularly appropriate to the *studieux*.

[2] Du Bellay seems to despise the epistle (cf. p. 115), a genre into which many of these poems appear to fit.

[3] Laum., vol. XV, p. 124. Cf. Laumonier's note: Marot seems a more likely source than Villon.

[4] Cf. Laum., vol. X, pp. 67, 146.

[5] Cf. Laum., vol. XVI, p. 345.　　　　　[6] Laum., vol. XV, pp. 16, 59.

poetry and the nature of the poet and, although he is 'malade
& grison', the Muse continues to appear, although more
rarely and leaving longer and longer intervals in between her
appearances, in which

> ... en lieu de vivre entre les Dieux,
> Je deviens homme à moy-mesme odieux.[1]

and he continues to follow (as he recommends his reader):
'ton Estre, ou ton Astre fatal'.[2]

However his poetry seems to have lost the fire and effer-
vescence of youth. The most characteristic example is *La
Salade*, which represents at its best the Ronsardian technique
of evolving a poem from a patchwork of reminiscences and
imitations of the poetry of predecessors, antique and native
French. This technique, common to all poets of the time,
is not necessarily conscious and deliberate.[3] Here, we have
a mixture of the rustic poem (highly realistic in detail, but retaining considerable dignity and not falling into the marotic),
the personal epistle and the didactic poem, teaching the lesson
of Nature and the way of life called the natural. The opening
of the poem lays particular emphasis on its real, experienced
background:

> Lave ta main blanche, gaillarde & nette,
> Suy mes talons, aporte une serviette,
> Allon cueillir la salade, & faison
> Part à noz ans des fruictz de la saison.
> D'un vague pas, d'une veuë escartée,
> Deçà delà jettée & rejettée,
> Or' sur la rive, ores sur un fossé,
> Or' sur un champ en paresse laissé

---

[1] Ibid., p. 21.   [2] Ibid., p. 26.

[3] Cf. J. Du Bellay's remarks on imitation in the preface to his second
edition of the *Olive*.

> Du laboureur, qui de luy-mesme aporte
> Sans cultiver herbes de toute sorte,
> Je m'en iray solitaire à l'escart.
>   Tu t'en iras, Jamyn, d'une autre part
> Chercher songneux, la boursette toffuë...[1]

Ronsard addresses his secretary, Amadis Jamyn, who was
with him during this period of illness spent at Saint-Côme
and elsewhere, and who, in his own poems, talks of similar
incidents and of Ronsard's activities as a country gentleman.
The action of the poem obviously takes place near 'ma belle
fonteine' and this is almost certainly the spring which is later
to be referred to as the 'fontaine d'Hélène'. The inference is
in fact that Ronsard and Jamyn are at Croixval, where many
springs flow near the bed of the tiny river Cendrine. Their
gathering of the salad is described in a tone of simple rustic
pedantry, sparkling with variety and, curiously enough,
fitting in admirably with the requirements of that most dignified type of poem, the epic, in which Ronsard advises the
poet to go at length into this very type of detail.[2] May there
be here a slight touch of raillery? Perhaps one may suggest
a comparison with the *Voyage d'Hercueil* and its continual
introduction of the word *saint* in contexts which are far from
holy, and in surroundings much more those of rustic drunken-
ness than poetic fury. Yet the whole of this 1569 collection
smacks of the light-hearted, and this irony, if such it is, is
incidental and not unexpected, amusing but dignified:

> Tu me diras que la fiebvre m'abuze,
> Que je suis fol, ma salade & ma Muse:
> Tu diras vray: je le veux estre aussy,
> Telle fureur me guarist mon soucy.

Thereupon Ronsard associates his poetic temperament

---

[1] Laum., vol. XV, p. 76 (Appendix, p. 151).
[2] Cf. also the beginning of the *Hylas* in this collection.

with a further *cliché* of Renaissance and earlier poetry: the
preference for the country life, free and peaceful, to the Court
life. In more general terms, he inveighs against 'nostre courte
& miserable vie' and then states man's defence against misery
and rising ambition, putting forward a number of authorities
advising rustic contentment in humble circumstances. This
cannot but remind us of Montaigne, in whose essays what is
experienced is invariably associated with what is read. Thus,
with Ronsard, the gathering of the salad produces a happiness
which is vastly reinforced by the reflection that this after all
is advised by the best authorities—in this case Virgil, Hesiod
and Horace. The poem is then rounded off in the same tone
in which it had begun, that of dramatic reality and everyday
humour:

> C'est trop presché: donne moy ma salade:
> El' ne vaut rien (dis-tu) pour un malade!
> He! quoy, Jamyn, tu fais le Medecin!
> Laisse moy vivre au moins jusqu'à la fin
> Tout à mon aise...

In general, this collection of poems stresses the note of
country domesticity. Its verse is amusing and unpretentious—
even wise, although the wisdom tends towards the commonplace[1] and the poet moves in the direction of the philosophy
of nature which Montaigne comes to in his later essays,
accepting the forces of destiny in association with those of
his own *nature* or *inclination*.[2]

We return to the *blason* with the poems describing the *Pin*,
the *Rossignol* and the *Soucy*. And here we are conscious of a
specific feeling that the demigods represent the hidden powers
of nature, and are a means of conveying plastically a vague
and even perhaps unorthodox belief in the mystery and magic

---

[1] Cf. Laum., vol. XV, p. 128.   [2] Cf. Cohen, vol. II, pp. 86, 391.

of her creation. The picture given in the *Pin* is exact and extremely alive:

> Quiconque soit qui eust embesongnée
> A te couper la premiere congnée,
> Avec le coup eust veu tout à la fois
> Jallir du sang...
> Chesne à Cérès, qui avoit en tout temps
> Le chef orné des bouquets du Printemps,
> Où la Dryade estoit dessous vivante,
> Naissant, mourant, tout ainsi que la plante.[1]

The poem, *Le Soucy*, brings with it another of the 'universalizing' morals which sum up so much of what Ronsard seems to feel about the living organism which is nature and creation:

> Te voyant naistre aussi tost que fanir,
> Soir et matin fay le moy souvenir
> Que nostre vie aux fleurettes resemble,
> Qui presque vit et presque meurt ensemble;...
> Si en naissant ce grand Maistre qui donne
> Heur et malheur à chacune personne,
> M'avoit donné, mon Cherouvrier, ta vois...
> Je chasserois la fiévre de mon corps
> Par le douceur de tant de beaux accords.
> En lieu d'avoir la nombreuse Musique,
> J'ay l'autre ardeur, la verve poëtique,
> Qui rompt ma fiévre, et charme mon souci;
> Ou, s'il n'est vray, je me console ainsi.[2]

But, from the point of view of the nature of the poet, perhaps the most interesting passage in these *Poèmes* occurs in the poem to Monsieur de Belot, later called *La Lyre*, in

[1] Cf. Cohen, vol. II, p. 367.
[2] Ibid., p. 366.

which Ronsard describes the effects on him of the ebb and flow of poetic fury and inspiration.[1]

It is clear that Ronsard, from 1569 onwards, starts from the idea of self-knowledge, proceeding from self-analysis and from a series of far from flattering self-portraits. To apply to this poetry the adjective 'personal' might be misleading unless it is realized that 'personal' poetry in the sixteenth century is the product of a certain imagination and rarely claims to be explicit introspection or the analysis of emotions belonging exclusively to a certain poet: it is an interest in an aesthetic pattern rather than in psychological self-portrayal. Even so, it emerges as legitimately personal in so far as this word has any meaning or value in literary criticism, and it can easily be demonstrated that, in Ronsard's poetry at this time, we can associate *nature*, poetry and biography, feeling, technique and expression.

Ronsard recognizes and accepts the presence of the fantastic and the furious within his own nature. Yet, as he says: 'souvent l'imaginer corrompt la verité',[2] and he desires to control the vagaries of the imagination because of a certain and perhaps a *natural* knowledge (for he has always possessed it, even in his early years) that the *media via* is best. Furthermore old age brings with it that desire for calm and tranquillity which is normal. Youth goes, and with it goes the time for fury. Indeed, at this time, Ronsard says farewell to the *Muses deslogées*[3] and compresses his doctrine of old age into a very few lines:

> J'ay varié ma vie en devidant la trame
> Que Clothon me filoit entre malade et sain:...

---

[1] Laum., vol. XV, pp. 18 ff.
[2] Cohen, vol. I, p. 912.
[3] Cf. ibid., pp. 817, 821. Cf. also p. 279.

> Le vray tresor de l'homme est la verte jeunesse,
> Le reste de nos ans ne sont que des hivers...
> Ne force ta nature, ains ensuy la raison...[1]

He retired to the country almost finally in 1575, with ten years of his life still to go—ten years in which he was to write very little indeed, for:

> Celuy qui devient vieil, matté d'un sang refroidy, peut bien dire à dieu aux Graces et aux Muses.[2]

In the country he became interested, as indeed he had been in 1569, in the life of the country gentleman, enjoying the sight of his flourishing garden[3] and leading an existence the usefulness and activity of which is borne witness to by Amadis Jamyn, his secretary, and Claude Binet, his biographer.[4] Even in the few begging poems which he published about this time,[5] he evidently believes he can afford to cultivate a certain bluff tone, a certain *liberté rustique*.[6] He takes advantage of his countryfiedness, of the righteousness and simplicity traditionally attached to the rustic life, to the *vie saine* so important to the writer.[7]

There are rustic elements even in the careful, courtly sonnets to Helen,[8] and there are realistic nature descriptions after 1569: witness especially the description of the song of the nightingale published in 1578:

> Il reprend, il retient, il recoupe le son
> Tantost haut, tantost bas, de sa longue chanson...[9]

---

[1] Cohen, vol. II, p. 634.   [2] Laum., vol. XVI, p. 345.

[3] Cf. the series of sonnets addressed to the *Duc de Touraine*: Cohen, vol. I, pp. 301 ff. Also vol. II, p. 542.

[4] Cf. Laum., vol. XV, p. 14.

[5] Cf. the *Bocage Royal*, especially the long poem to Henri III published in 1584.

[6] Cohen, vol. I, p. 800.   [7] Cf. Ficino: *Les trois livres...*, p. 51.

[8] Cf. Cohen, vol. I, pp. 230, 232, 246.   [9] Cohen, vol. II, p. 50.

The song of the nightingale belongs to a long tradition, and Ronsard describes it often, in emulation of Pliny, of Pierre Belon and of Peletier du Mans, in whose verse the bird:

> Declique un li clicitis
> Tretis petit fetis...[1]

in the manner of the songs set to music by Jannequin. In 1555, Ronsard's imitation of the nightingale had been less harsh and less merely onomatopoeic:

> Si tost que tu as beu quelque peu de rosée,
> Soit de nuict, soit de jour, caché dans un buisson,
> Pendant les æsles bas tu dis une chanson
> D'une notte rustique à ton gré composée.[2]

In 1569, curiously, it is much more medieval:

> ... t'esclatant d'une voix qui gringote
> Ores en haute, ores en basse note,
> A bec ouvert, d'un siffletis trenchant,
> Hachant, coupant, entre-rompant ton chant
> De cent fredons...[3]

But this apparent increase in realism is not paralleled in other examples of the poet's descriptive writing such as the elegy on the cutting down of part of the *Forêt de Gâtine* which is anything but realistic in tone. He continues to attach great importance to choice and variety, expressing this in an image typical of the century: that of the bee gathering pollen from a variety of flowers. He also uses the image of the bouquet of flowers gathered selectively. The argument is relatively unimportant, although the idea of the poetic fable persists, and the order of the poems is one belonging, not to logic, but to poetic fantasy and the poetic temperament or *naturel*.[4]

---

[1] *L'Amour des Amours* (1555), p. 126. [2] Laum., vol. VII, p. 266.
[3] Cohen, vol. II, p. 371. [4] Cf. Cohen, vol. I, p. 346.

This is 'une naifve & naturelle poesie' [1] and the poetic flowers
are subordinate to the idea of an imaginative whole. Variety
and riches are organized within a unity and decoration, technique and care go hand in hand with order, with *prevoyance*
and *naturel jugement*. All this corresponds to the *nature* of
Ronsard the poet as he understands it at this time, and even
in the 1587 preface to the *Franciade*, addressed as it is to the
lecteur apprentif, Ronsard cannot forbear to bring in the
nature of man:

> ceste lamentable plainte de Mezance sur le corps mort de son fils
> Lauzus, & mille autres telles ecstatiques descriptions... lesquelles
> te feront Poëte... & t'irriteront les naifves & naturelles scintilles
> de l'ame que dès la naissance tu as receues... car tout homme
> dès le naistre reçoit en l'ame je ne sçay quelles fatales impressions,
> qui le contraignent suivre plustost son Destin que sa volonté.[2]

Finally, the poet puts aside even love in favour of wisdom.
But then Ronsard never seriously followed the example of
so many neoplatonic poets in regarding love as a means to
knowledge. He found his wisdom through meditation, not
forgetting the simple pleasures of the rural life, but rather
transmuting them, making them artificial and placing them
in a picture:

> Car seul maistre de moy j'allois plein de loisir,
> Où le pied me portoit, conduit de mon desir,
> Ayant tousjours és mains pour me servir de guide
> Aristote ou Platon, ou le docte Euripide,...
> Puis du livre ennuyé, je regardois les fleurs,...
> Ne me pouvant saouler, ainsi qu'en un tableau,
> D'admirer la Nature, et ce qu'elle a de beau,
> Et de dire en parlant aux fleurettes escloses,
> Celuy est presque Dieu qui cognoist toutes choses,
> Esloigné du vulgaire, et loin des courtisans...[3]

---

[1] Laum., vol. XVI, p. 334.   [2] Ibid., p. 333.
[3] Cohen, vol. I, p. 276. Cf. Appendix, p. 160.

In this passage we have that curiously qualified enthusiasm for solitude in the midst of nature which is so typical of the sixteenth century in France. Le Caron, for example, uses the conventional pastoral beginning to his dialogues, with a mention of his father's house and garden, 'lieu autant propre à la delectation philosophique qu'à touts autres plaisirs...' [1] Jean de la Taille gives us a notable example of this type of description in the first few lines of his *Courtisan retiré*.[2] In the work of Ronsard himself Nature never loses those aspects—fertility, agriculture, country sports, even gardening and ornamental cultivation and grottoes—which bind her to man. Thus he loves above all: 'jardins qui sentent le sauvage',[3] and in his sonnets to Marie, he haunts: 'quelque jardin pres d'un bois solitere'.[4] With all her Petrarchan wildernesses, Nature is rarely thinkable for the poet apart from man, and if the idea of a Rousseauesque solitude does intrude, it is fleetingly and seems to indicate again a grasping at variety. As Charles de Sainte-Marthe puts it:

> apres longue frequentation des fructueuses & bien cultivés Ver-giers, l'asperité & solitude des boys nous agrée, tant nous est la Nature par sa diverse varieté non moins belle qu'aymable.[5]

It is in this nature, full of the presence of men, or occasionally of demigods, more frequently of reading and literary reminiscences, that the poet is subject to that melancholy spirit which, by a strange process, controls fury:

> tant vault la meditation, qui par longueur de temps les engendre en un esprit melancholique, quand la bride de la contrainte arreste & refreint la premiere course impetueuse des fureurs & monstrueuses imaginations de l'esprit, à l'exemple des grandes

---

[1] *Dialogues*, f. 150. [2] Cf. pp. 46, 55 of *La Famine...* (Paris, 1573).
[3] Laum., vol. XI, p. 144. [4] Ibid., vol. VII, p. 184.
[5] *Poèsie françoise* (Paris, 1540), p. 4.

rivieres qui bouillonnent, escument & fremissent à l'entour de leurs rempars, où, quand elles courent la plaine sans contrainte, elles marchent lentement & paresseusement, sans frapper les rivages ny d'escumes ny de bruit.[1]

This passage from the preface to the *Franciade*, published in 1587, might well be seen as a summary of Ronsard's poetic career, from the occasionally unpleasantly exaggerated furies of the pindaric odes of his earlier years to the quieter, broader poems of his later years which, although they have been called *baroque*, are certainly not so in the same sense as Malherbe's *Larmes de Saint Pierre*, or indeed as Ronsard's own *Ode à Michel de l'Hospital*. But, whatever the relation of this passage to Ronsard's life, its application to the theory of poetry is clear. First Nature and observation and contemplation, then meditation and imagination, finally the lengthy burgeoning, the emotion recollected in tranquillity.

[1] Laum., vol. XVI, p. 348.

CHAPTER V

Nature and the Poet

WE are urged by many critics to regard Ronsard, the poet of nature, as a realistic poet describing the simple everyday life and scenes of the countryside. It is true that he does display considerable knowledge even of the less attractive aspects of the countryman's life, when, for example, he talks of the callouses of the ploughman and the vinegrower, the stupidity of the peasant, the gloominess of the *antre* and so forth. Again Laumonier suggests that his descriptions of the dances of the demigods are based on natural realities, that the *cottes* of the dancing Nymphs are the mists that rise in the evening over the *Vendômois* meadows.[1]

This last theory is attractive in its simplicity, but we prefer to see these dances as one of many natural symbols used by the poet. The Nymphs replace the realities of nature which the poet undoubtedly observed and the imagination, as so frequently happens, dominates and overwhelms the memory, the object itself being secondary to the feeling it arouses in the poet.

In general, the poetry of the later Renaissance in France is not realistic but decorative. Art is invoked rather than life, an art which, for Ronsard, is based on the invention and the imagination which transpose, or, better, transmute the real, for poets:

d'une petite cassine font un magnifique Palais, qu'ils enrichissent,

---

[1] Laum., vol. XII, p. 48, note 2.

dorent & embellissent par le dehors de marbre, Jaspe & Porphire, de guillochis, ovalles, frontispices & piedestals, frises & chapiteaux... Apres ils adjoustent vergers & jardins, compartimens & larges allees...[1]

The main means used by the poet to achieve this end of imaginative description is metaphor. And his use of this figure is amply explained by Antoine Fouquelin in his *Rhétorique françoise*:

> On peut aussi deriver des metaphores des animaulx & choses qui ont ame, comme des plantes & arbres: comme en la traduction Charicles est soudain venue en fleur de beauté & parfaite vigueur:
>
> Ronsart en ses amours:
>
>> Aussi ne l'or qui peut tentér
>> Ni autre grace, ni maintien,
>> Ne sçauroient en mon cœur entér
>> Un autre portrait que le tien...

> Les Rheteurs admonestent, que le premier lieu est deu à ces Metaphores, qui tumbent dessous les sentimens, principalement des yeus, le quel est le plus vif de tous... Parquoy Aristote louë entre toutes les autres ces Metaphores lesquelles frapent les yeus, par la clarté de leur signification... Mais principalement ce Trope plait, quand quelque sens & mouvement est baillé aus choses inanimees, comme s'ils avoient une ame...[2]

In the same way, nature is important to Ronsard not as existence but as movement: it is valuable because it possesses vitality. *Natura naturata*, or the details of Nature's creation, are not a Chaos but an assembly of vital forces under the dominant controlling force of *natura naturans*. These metaphors full of movement and *soul* are perhaps a reflection of

[1] Laum., vol. XVI, p. 340.   [2] *Rhétorique*, pp. 17 ff.

the idea of the poetic fable. Here the poet's work is analogous to that of Nature as he creates figures of speech and:

> autres semblables atomes, par lesquels j'ai composé le petit monde de mes inventions.[1]

From eloquence and rhetoric with their apparently easily definable rules and habits, we are forced to descend into the marshy ground of emotion and sensibility. Eloquence implies emotion. Even in the *Deffence et Illustration*, with all its emphasis upon hard work and scholarly discipline, Du Bellay is constrained to say: 'Celuy est vrayment poete... qui tiendra la bride de mes passions.' [2] And we are forced away from the description, with its easily analysed component parts, to the evocation of a mood or emotion in the mind of the reader, a thing which cannot be done merely by presenting reality as it stands and which is not merely description. Through the imitation of the world as it appears there shines the temperament of the poet, not only his emotions but also what we can only call the pattern of his mind.

Ronsard's temperament is primarily dualistic. As a Saturnian poet he is invaded alternately by inspiration and spleen or melancholy. Similarly his life is divided between Court and country: this fact has perhaps something to do with the continual reappearance in his poetry of the literary convention opposing Court and country life.[3] In fact, the whole idea of natural wisdom in Ronsard's didactic poetry can be traced back to this medieval controversy and, of course, to various passages of Latin poetry which handle the same theme (Horace and Virgil spring to mind immediately).

Ronsard never appears as a real solitary. His excursions

---

[1] Laum., vol. I, p. 55.   [2] *Deffence et Illustration*, p. 179.
[3] Laum., vol. X, p. 77.

into the country are frequently a relief from study or love
and are rarely contemplative:

> J'ay l'esprit tout ennuié
> D'avoir trop estudié
> Les Phenomenes d'Arate:
> Il est tans que je m'ébate
> Et que j'aille aus chams joüer.[1]

He is much more eager for country sports, and his contemplation of nature is often closely allied to action: he is too
nervous and too little settled to be an ideal contemplator. He
is not entirely different from the soldier he was destined to
become in his youth and, like Montaigne, he finds too long
meditation beyond him. His imagination is fitful and follows
the will o' the wisp of his fury. Country solitude must be
followed by the life of the Court, even quite late on in his life.

Similarly, although Ronsard uses once only the commonplace contrast between Nature *mère* and *marâtre*,[2] the balance
between the two is nevertheless implicit in the poet's whole
attitude to Nature, now the joyous, fertile nature of the *Vendômois*, now the single flower which droops and dies. Both
these are the law of Nature, for 'Amour et mort est une même
chose' and all existence partakes of life and death. Even in a
country picnic:

> Tousjours avec la lyesse,
> La tristesse
> Se mesle segrettement.[3]

Seen as a whole, the poetry of Ronsard suggests in itself a
deliberate desire for dualism. To use Laumonier's terms, there
is a continual succession of *grave* and *léger*. That this was a
novelty at this time is certainly implied by Ronsard in the

[1] Laum., vol. VI, p. 105.   [2] Laum., vol. X, p. 75.
[3] Laum., vol III, p. 217.

following lines from a preface published in 1563: '...tu trouveras estrange, que... je change si soubdain de façon d'escrire, faisant imprimer en ce livre autres nouvelles compositions, toutes diferentes de stille & d'argument de celles que durant les troubles j'avois mises en lumiere.'[1] Is it an exaggeration to see this as a transposition of Ronsard's attitude towards the world and his philosophy of the universe? Is there not a parallel between this type of poetic composition and the *loy de nature?* Variety for the poet is indeed here a series of extremes rather than a shaded palette of *nuances*, and this is in general agreement with the Renaissance picture of the universe and its scientific explanations, in terms of reactions and oppositions of one thing to another.[2] Nature is seen to be a power controlling and keeping in a type of equilibrium a number of forces which are themselves in continual movement. Apart from these forces, which belong to the physical world, there are others, in the main allegorical in their expression and belonging to the moral world. All these forces appear in Ronsard's poetry as plastic creations, but the emphasis is upon myth and symbol rather than on allegory.[3] Variety is an essential part of the picture and, although the poet gives Nature no powers which might be described as magical, he represents her as a background frieze which is continually alive and in movement. The invention and imagination natural to the poet, together with his learning and observation, produce canvases which transcend the real and the everyday. Yet Ronsard is decided not to 'extravaguer comme un frenetique' and although he abandons the *classical* order of *Mignonne, allon voir...* in his longer poems (especially after about 1555), he replaces it by another type of order

[1] Laum., vol. XII, p. 3.
[2] Cf. *inter alia*: L. Le Roy: *De la Vicissitude des choses* (Paris, 1575).
[3] This tendency being of course one typical of the Renaissance.

which has been variously described as *baroque*, imaginative and even (in the vocabulary of Ramus) as *prudent*.

All this is highly conscious, for the poet, like Nature herself, is ingenious and full of *artifice*. The ideals of the neo-platonists are treated with realism: poetic fury and divine inspiration is a poetic theme and corresponds to a passing rather than a constant state, having to be allied with learning and bringing with it certain temperamental disadvantages, the most obvious of which is melancholy.

As Ronsard grows older, the 'furious' ideals of his youth recede somewhat and he sees a place for the ideas of amusement and *soulagement* which his century, after all, considered to be part of the poet's normal make-up and which are so often celebrated by Du Bellay and others. Ronsard realizes the fragility of the poet's *nature*, to which he is all the time determined to submit himself. And finally he finds room in his poetry for a type of attitude to living which makes an excellent conclusion to an essay, but whose importance in Ronsard's predominantly artistic and aesthetic poetry must not be over-emphasized. This natural philosophy, as one may well call it, is based upon the acceptance of *nature* as an innate and positive good, upon the contemplation of the whole of the universe and upon a realization that the way of nature is a middle way. This is not merely a return to the didactic note of the early part of the century. Being careful not to omit the real, the sensual pleasures of the countryside and its sports, Ronsard claims a type of wisdom and nourishment for one who studies Nature, absorbs her and indeed is a part of her:

> Six ans estoient coulez, et la septiesme annee
> Estoit presques entiere en ses pas retournee,
> Quand loin d'affection, de desir et d'amour,
> En pure liberté je passois tout le jour,

Et franc de tout soucy qui les ames devore,
Je dormois dés le soir jusqu'au point de l'aurore...
Puis du livre ennuyé, je regardois les fleurs,
Fueilles, tiges, rameaux, especes et couleurs,
Et l'entrecoupement de leurs formes diverses,
Peintes de cent façons, jaunes, rouges et perses,
Ne me pouvant saouler, ainsi qu'en un tableau,
D'admirer la Nature, et ce qu'elle a de beau,
Et de dire en parlant aux fleurettes escloses,
Celuy est presque Dieu qui cognoist toutes choses,...
J'aimois le cours suivy d'une longue riviere,
Et voir onde sur onde allonger sa carriere,
Et flot à l'autre flot en roulant s'attacher,
Et pendu sur le bord me plaisoit d'y pescher,
Estant plus resjouy d'une chasse muette
Troubler des escaillez la demeure secrette,
Tirer avecq' la ligne en tramblant emporté
Le credule poisson prins a l'haim apasté,
Qu'un grand Prince n'est aise avant prins à la chasse
Un cerf qu'en haletant tout un jour il pourchasse...[1]

Here the poet is 'en pure liberté', he is free from love and care and in possession of his own self, his *nature*. Reading, observation, action, each brings its own contribution to wisdom and knowledge in the midst of a natural *décor* whose solitude is *peinturez* and whose waters move according to a definite pattern as do the stars in the sky. All things—even love and Hélène—are subject to Nature.

This is the wisdom the poet teaches—that which comes naturally through reading and contemplation, activities recommended and emphasized by Ficino, Le Roy, Mesmes and many other Renaissance writers, for the contemplation of the greater aspects of Nature is an essential beginning to all

[1] Cohen, vol. I, p. 276 (Appendix, p. 160).

discovery and knowledge. This is not the moral common-places of the fifteenth and earlier centuries, but a much more direct form of knowledge. Ramus defines the task of the poet and orator as follows:

> la verité des choses comprises es ars est ainsi naturellement pro-posée a l'esprit, comme est la couleur a la veüe: & ce que nous appellons enseigner, n'est pas bailler la sapience, ains seulement tourner & diriger l'esprit a contempler ce que de soy mesme il eut peu apercevoir, s'il se fut là tourné & dirigeé.[1]

Le Roy suggests that this knowledge will come most easily through the sense of sight:

> Par ce que tous naturellement desirent sçavoir choses nouvelles... cherissans entre les sens principalement la veue & l'ouye... Mais la veue plus: dont a procedé le commencement de science par admiration. Car voyans le ciel, le soleil, la lune, & autres estoilles... ils s'appliquerent à contempler la disposition du monde, & rechercher les secrets de nature.[2]

Rosamund Tuve, in her *Elizabethan and Metaphysical Imagery*, suggests that in so-called didactic writings of this period the writer is particularly preoccupied by the 'imagina-tive ordering of reality',[3] for, as Puttenham has it, by the imagination

> are represented unto the soule all manner of bewtifull visions, whereby the inventive parte of the mynde is so much holpen, as without it no man could devise any new or rare thing.

And so it is with Ronsard. We are all the time conscious of coming upon pictures and images based upon the observation of nature which indicate to the reader the pattern of the

---

[1] *Dialectique*, pp. 1 ff.

[2] *De la Vicissitude*, p. 27.

[3] R. Tuve: *Elizabethan and Metaphysical Imagery* (Chicago, 1947), p. 392.

universe as it is discovered and selected by the poet. For the didactic is also the beautiful and the pleasant. Harmonious beauty and the beauty of *accordans discords* both play a part, for the work of a poet displays a view of the whole of the universe. Thus all is grist to the poet's and to the reader's mill. Everything that the poet proposes is knowledge, especially and most seriously valid if he keeps to what can be held within the sphere of nature, a sphere embracing all things yet essentially undefined.

Appendix

I

LES LOUANGES DE VANDOMOIS

à Julien Peccate

ODE

O terre fortunée
Des Muses le sejour,
Que le ciel, & l'année
Serénent d'un beau jour.

En toi, de main non chiche
L'abondance et bon heur
Ont de leur corne riche
Renversé tout l'honneur.

Deus longs tertres t'emmurent,
Dont les flancs durs & fors
Des fiers vents qui murmurent
S'opposent aus effors.

Sur l'un Gâtine sainte
Mere des demidieus,
Sa teste de verd painte,
Envoie jusque aus cieus,

129

Et sur l'autre prend vie
Maint beau sep, dont le vin
Porte bien peu d'envie
Au vignoble Angevin.

Le Loir tard à la fuite
En soi s'ebanoiant,
D'eau lentement conduite
Tes champs va tournoiant,

Rendant bon & fertile
Le pais traversé,
Par l'humeur qui distile
Du gras limon versé.

Bien qu'on n'i vienne querre
Par flots injurieus,
De l'Atlantique terre
L'or tant laborieus,

Et la Gemme arrachée
Des boiaus d'un rocher,
Ne soit point là cherchée
Par l'avare nocher:

L'Inde pourtant ne pense
La vaincre, car les Dieus
D'une autre recompense
La fortunent bien mieus.

La justice grand erre
S'enfuiant d'ici bas,
Laissa dans nostre terre
Le saint trac de ses pas.

Et s'encore à cette heure
De l'antique saison
Quelque vertu demeure,
C'est bien là sa maison.

Les Muses honorées,
Les Muses mon souci,
Et les Graces dorées
I habitent aussi,

Et tes Nimphes natives
Citoiennes des bois,
Qui au caquet des rives
Font acorder leurs vois,

Chantant de bonne grace
Les faits & les honneurs
De la celeste race
Des Bourbons nos seigneurs.

Bref quelque part que j'erre
Tant le ciel me soit dous,
Ce petit coin de terre
Me rira par sus tous.

Là je veil que la Parque
Tranche mon fatal fil,
Et m'envoie en la barque
De perdurable exil.

Là, te faudra repandre
Russeaus de pleurs, parmi
La vaine & froide çendre
De Ronsard ton ami.[1]

[1] Laum., vol. I, p. 221. First published as Ode XVII of Book II of the
Quatre premiers livres des odes (Paris, 1550).

II

A LA FONTAINE BELLERIE

ODE

Argentine fonteine vive
De qui le beau cristal courant,
D'une fuite lente, & tardive
Ressuscite le pré mourant,

Quand l'esté ménager moissonne
Le sein de Ceres devétu,
Et l'aire par compas resonne
Dessous l'épi de blé batu.

A tout jamais puisses-tu estre
En honneur, & religion
Au beuf, & au bouvier champestre
De ta voisine region.

Et la lune d'un œil prospere
Voie les bouquins amenans
La Nimphe aupres de ton repere
Un bal sur l'herbe demenans,

Comme je desire fonteine
De plus ne songer boire en toi
L'esté, lors que la fievre ameine
La mort dépite contre moi.[1]

[1] Laum., vol. II, p. 14. First published as Ode VI of Book III of the *Quatre premiers livres des odes* (Paris, 1550).

III

Saincte Gastine, heureuse secretaire
 De mes ennuis, qui respons en ton bois,
 Ores en haulte, ores en basse voix,
 Aux longz souspirs que mon cuœur ne peult taire:
Loyr, qui refrains la course voulontaire
 Du plus courant de tes flotz vandomoys,
 Quand acuser ceste beaulté tu m'ois,
 De qui tousjours je m'affame & m'altere:
Si dextrement l'augure j'ay receu,
 Et si mon œil ne fut hyer deceu
 Des doulx regardz de ma doulce Thalie,
Dorenavant poëte me ferez,
 Et par la France appellez vous serez,
 L'un mon laurier, l'aultre ma Castalie.[1]

[1] Laum., vol. IV, p. 128. First published as Sonnet CXXXII of *Les Amours* (Paris, 1552).

IV

ODE

Quand je suis vint ou trente mois
Sans retourner en Vandomois,
Plein de pensées vagabondes,
Plein d'un remors, & d'un souci,
Aus rochers je me plains ainsi,
Aus bois, aus antres, & aus ondes.

   Rochers, bien que soiés agés
De trois mil ans, vous ne changés
Jamais ni d'estat ni de forme,
Mais toujours ma jeunesse fuit,
Et la vieillesse qui me suit
De jeune en vieillard me transforme.

   Bois, bien que perdiés tous les ans
En l'hiver vos cheveus plaisans,
L'an d'apres, qui se renouvelle,
Renouvelle aussi vôtre chef,
Mais le mien ne peut derechef
R'avoir sa perruque nouvelle.

   Antres, je me suis veu chés vous
Avoir jadis verds les genous,
Le cors habille, & la main bonne,
Mais ores j'ai le cors plus dur,
Et les genous, que n'est le mur
Qui froidement vous environne.

   Ondes, sans fin vous promenés,
Et vous menés & ramenés
Vos flots d'un cours qui ne sejourne,
Et moi, sans faire long sejour,

Je m'en vais de nuit & de jour,
Mais comme vous je ne retourne.
   Si esse que je ne voudrois
Avoir esté ni roc, ni bois,
Antre, ni onde, pour defendre
Mon cors contre l'age emplumé,
Car ainsi dur, je n'eusse aimé
Toi qui m'as fait vieillir, Cassandre.[1]

---

[1] Laum., vol. VII, p. 98. First published as Ode XIII of Book IV of the *Quatre premiers livres des odes* (Paris, 1555).

K

V

ODE

Bel aubepin verdissant,
Fleurissant
Le long de ce beau rivage,
Tu es vestu jusqu'au bas
Des longs bras
D'une lambrunche sauvage.

Deux camps drillantz de fourmis
Se sont mis
En garnison soubz ta souche:
Et dans ton tronc mi-mangé
Arangé
Les avettes ont leur couche.

Le gentil rossignolet
Nouvelet,
Avecque sa bien aymée,
Pour ses amours aleger
Vient loger
Tous les ans en ta ramée:

Dans laquelle il fait son ny
Bien garny
De laine & de fine soye,
Où ses petitz s'eclorront,
Qui seront
De mes mains la douce proye.

Or' vy gentil aubepin,
Vy sans fin,
Vy sans que jamais tonnerre,
Ou la congnée, ou les vens,
Ou les tems
Te puissent ruer par terre.[1]

[1] Laum., vol. VII, p. 242. First published in the *Nouvelle continuation des amours* (Paris, 1556).

VI

HYMNE DE L'ÉTERNITÉ

A MADAME MARGARITE,
SEUR UNICQUE DU ROY

Remply d'un feu divin qui m'a l'ame eschauffée,
Je veux mieux que jamais, suivant les pas d'Orphée,
Decouvrir les secretz de Nature & des Cieux,
Recherchez d'un esprit qui n'est poinct ocieux:
Je veux, s'il m'est possible, attaindre à la louange
De celle qui jamais pour les ans ne se change,
Mais bien qui faict changer les siecles & les temps,
Les moys, & les saisons & les jours inconstans,
Sans jamais se muer, pour n'estre poinct sujecte,
Comme Royne & maistresse, à la loy qu'ell' a faicte.
L'œuvre est grand & fascheux, mais le desir que j'ay
D'attenter un grand faict, m'en convye à l'essay:
Puis je le veux donner à une qui merite,
Qu'avec l'Eternité sa gloire soit escrite.

  Donne moy donc de grace, immense Eternité,
Pouvoir de raconter ta grande deité,
Donne l'archet d'airain, & la lyre ferrée,
D'acier donne la corde, & la voix acérée,
Afin que ma chanson dure aussy longuement
Que tu dures au Ciel perpetuellement:
Toy la Royne des ans, des siecles, & de l'aage,
Qui as eu pour ton lot tout le Ciel en partage,
La premiere des Dieux, où bien loing du soucy,
Et de l'humain travail qui nous tourmente icy,
Par toy mesme contente, & par toy bien heureuse,
Sans rien faire tu vis en tous biens plantureuse.

Tout au plus hault du Ciel dans un throsne doré,
Tu te siedz en l'abit d'un manteau coloré
De pourpre rayé d'or, duquel la borderie
De tous costez s'esclatte en riche pierrerie.
Et là, tenant au poing un grand sceptre aimantin,
Tu ordonnes tes loix au severe Destin,
Qu'il n'ose oultrepasser, & que luy mesme engrave
Fermes au front du Ciel, ainsi qu'à toy esclave,
Faisant tourner soubz toy les neuf temples voultez,
Qui dedans & dehors cernent de tous costez,
Sans rien laisser ailleurs, tous les membres du monde,
Qui gist dessoubz tes piedz comme une boulle ronde.
   A ton dextre costé la Jeunesse se tient,
Jeunesse au chef crespu, dont la tresse luy vient
Flottant jusqu' aux talons par ondes non tondue,
Qui luy frappe le doz en filz d'or estendue:
Cette Jeunesse ayant le teint de roses franc,
D'une boucle d'azur ceinte de sur le flanc,
Dans un vase doré te donne de la dextre
A boire du nectar, afin de te faire estre
Tousjours saine & disposte, & afin que ton front
Ne soit jamais ridé comme les nostres sont.
De l'aultre main senestre, avec grande rudesse
Repoulse l'estomac de la triste Vieillesse,
Et la chasse du Ciel à coups de poing, afin
Que le Ciel ne vieillisse, & qu'il ne prenne fin.
A ton aultre costé la Puissance eternelle
Se tient debout plantée, armée à la mammelle
D'un corselet gravé qui luy couvre le sein,
Branlant de nuict & jour une espée en la main,
Pour tenir en seurté les bordz de ton empire,
Ton regne & ta richesse, afin qu'elle n'empire
Par la fuitte des ans, & pour donner la mort
A quiconque vouldroit favoriser Discord,
Discord ton ennemy, qui ses forces assemble
Pour faire mutiner les Elementz ensemble

A la perte du Monde, & de ton doulx repos,
Et vouldroit, s'il pouvoit, rengendrer le cahos.
Mais tout incontinent que cet ennemy brasse
Trahison contre toy, la Vertu le menasse,
Et l'envoye là bas aux abysmes d'Enfer,
Garroté piedz & mains de cent liens de fer.

 Bien loing derriere toy, mais bien loing par derriere,
La Nature te suit, Nature bonne mere,
D'un baston appuyée, à qui mesmes les Dieux
Font honneur du genoil quand elle vient aux Cieux.

 Saturne apres la suict, le vieillard venerable,
Marchant tardivement, dont la main honorable,
Bien que vieille & ridée, eleve une grand faulx
Où les Heures vont d'ordre à grandz pas tous egaulx,
Et l'An qui tant de fois tourne, passe & repasse,
Glissant d'un pied certain par une mesme trace.

 O grande Eternité, merveilleux sont tes faictz!
Tu nourris l'univers en eternelle paix,
D'un lien aimantin les siecles tu attaches,
Et dessoubz ton grand sein tout ce monde tu caches,
Luy donnant vie & force, aultrement il n'auroit
Membres, ame, ne vie, & confuz periroit:
Mais ta vive vertu le conserve en son estre
Tousjours entier & sain sans amoindrir ne croistre.

 Tu n'as pas les humains favorisez ainsy,
Que tu as heritez de peine & de soucy,
De vieillesse & de mort, qui est leur vray partage,
Faisant bien peu de cas de tout nostre lignage,
Qui ne peult conserver sa generation
Sinon par le succés de reparation,
A laquelle Venus incite la Nature
Par plaisir mutuel de chaque creature
A garder son espece, & tousjours restaurer
Sa race qui ne peut eternelle durer:
Mais toy sans restaurer ton estre & ton essence,
Vivant tu te soustiens de ta propre·puissance,

Sans rien craindre la mort, car le cruel trespas
Ne regne point au Ciel comme il regne icy bas,
Le lieu de son empire, où maling il exerce
Par mille estranges mortz sa malice diverse,
N'ayant non plus d'esgard aux Princes qu'aux Bouviers,
Pesle mesle egallant les sceptres aux leviers.

    La grand trouppe des Dieux qui là hault environne
Tes flancz, comme une belle & plaisante couronne,
Quand elle parle à toy ne dict point il sera,
Il fut, ou telle chose ou telle se fera,
C'est à faire aux humains à dire telle chose:
Sans plus le temps present devant toy se repose
Et se sied à tes piedz: car tout le temps passé
Et celluy qui n'est pas encores advancé
Sont presens à ton œil, qui d'un seul clin regarde
Le passé, le present, & cestuy là qui tarde
A venir quant à nous, & non pas quant à toy,
Ny à ton œil qui voit tous les temps davant soy.

    Nous aultres journalliers, nous perdons la memoire
Des temps qui sont passez, & si ne pouvons croire
Ceux qui sont à venir, comme estans imperfaictz,
Et d'une masse brute inutilement faictz,
Aveuglez & perclus de la saincte lumiere,
Que le peché perdit en nostre premier pere:
Mais ferme tu retiens dedans ton souvenir
Tout ce qui est passé, & ce qui doibt venir,
Comme haulte Deesse eternelle, & perfaicte,
Et non ainsy que nous de masse impure faicte.

    Tu es toute dans toy, ta partie, & ton tout,
Sans nul commencement, sans meillieu, ne sans bout,
Invincible, immuable, entiere, & toute ronde,
N'ayant partie en toy, qui dans toy ne responde,
Toute commencement, toute fin, tout meillieu,
Sans tenir aucun lieu, de toutes choses lieu,
Qui fais ta deité du tout par tout estandre,
Qu'on imagine bien, & qu'on ne peult comprendre.

Je te salu' Deesse au grand œil tout-voyant,
Mere du grand Olympe au grand tour flamboyant,
Grande mere des Dieux, grande Royne & Princesse:
(Si je l'ay merité) concede moy, Deesse,
Concede moy ce don, c'est qu'apres mon trespas
(Ayant laissé pourrir ma depouille çà bas)
Je puisse voyr au ciel la belle Margarite,
Pour qui j'ay ta louange en cet hymne descrite.[1]

[1] Laum., vol. VIII, p. 246. First published in the *Second livre des Hymnes* (Paris, 1556).

VII

ELEGIE

de Pierre de Ronsard
à J. Grevin

GREVIN, en tous mestiers on peult estre parfaict:
Par longue experience un advocat est faict
Excellent en son art, & celuy qui pratique
Dessus les corps humains un art Hippocratique:
Le sage Philosophe, & le grave Orateur,
Et celuy qui se dit des nombres inventeur
Par estude est sçavant: mais non pas le Poëte,
«Car la Muse icy bas ne fut jamais parfaicte,
Ny ne sera, GREVIN: la haulte Deité
Ne veult pas tant d'honneur à nostre humanité
Imparfaicte & grossiere: & pource elle n'est dine
De la perfection d'une fureur divine.

Le don de Poësie est semblable à ce feu,
Lequel aux nuicts d'hyver comme un presage est veu
Ores dessus un fleuve, ores sur une prée,
Ores dessus le chef d'une forest sacrée,
Sautant & jallissant, jettant de toutes pars
Par l'obscur de la nuict de grans rayons espars:
Le peuple le regarde, & de frayeur & crainte
L'ame luy bat au corps, voyant la flame saincte.
A la fin la clarté de ce grand feu descroist,
Devient palle & blaffart, & plus il n'apparoist:
En un mesme pays jamais il ne sejourne,
Et au lieu dont il part jamais il ne retourne:
Il saute sans arrest de cartier en cartier,
Et jamais un païs de luy n'est heritier,

143

Ains il se communique, & sa flame est montrée
(Où moins on l'esperoit) en une autre contrée.
    Ainsi ny les Hebreux, les Grecs, ny les Romains
N'ont eu la Poësie entiere entre leurs mains:
Elle a veu l'Allemagne, & a pris accroissance
Aux rives d'Angleterre, en Escosse, et en France,
Sautant deçà delà, & prenant grand plaisir
En estrange païs divers hommes choisir,
Rendant de ses rayons la province allumée,
Mais bien tost sa lumiere en l'air est consumée.
«La louange n'est pas tant seulement à un,
«De tous elle est hostesse, & visite un chacun,
«Et sans avoir égard aux biens ny à la race,
«Favorisant chacun, un chacun elle embrasse.
    Quant à moy, mon GREVIN, si mon nom espandu
S'enfle de quelque honneur, il m'est trop cher vendu,
Et ne sçay pas comment un autre s'en contente:
Mais je sçay que mon art grevement me tourmente,
Encore que, moy vif, je jouysse du bien
Qu'on donne apres la mort au mort qui ne sent rien.
Car pour avoir gousté les ondes de Permesse
Je suis tout aggravé de somme & de paresse,
Inhabile, inutile: & qui pis, je ne puis
Arracher cest humeur dont esclave je suis.
    Je suis opiniastre, indiscret, fantastique,
Farouche, soupçonneux, triste & melancolicque,
Content & non content, mal propre, & mal courtois:
Au reste craignant Dieu, les princes & les lois,
Né d'assez bon esprit, de nature assez bonne,
Qui pour rien ne voudroit avoir faché personne:
Voylà mon naturel, mon GREVIN, & je croy
Que tous ceux de mon art ont tels vices que moy.
    Pour me recompenser, au moins si Calliope
M'avoit faict le meilleur des meilleurs de sa trope,
Et si j'estois en l'art qu'elle enseigne parfait,
De tant de passions je seroy satisfait:

Mais me voyant sans plus icy demy Poëte,
Un mestier moins divin que le mien je souhaitte.

Deux sortes il y a de mestier sur le mont
Où les neuf belles Seurs leurs demeurances font:
L'un favorise à ceux qui riment & composent,
Qui les vers par leur nombre arrengent & disposent
Et sont du nom de vers dicts versificateurs,
Ils ne sont que de vers seulement inventeurs,
Froids, gelez & glacez, qui en naissant n'apportent
Sinon un peu de vie, en laquelle ils avortent:
Ils ne servent de rien qu'à donner des habits
A la cannelle, au succre, au gingembre, & au ris:
Ou si, par trait de temps, ils forcent la lumiere,
Si est-ce que sans nom ils demeurent derriere,
Et ne sont jamais leus, car Phebus Apollon
Ne les a point touchez de son aspre éguillon.
Ils sont comme apprentis, lesquels n'ont peu atteindre
A la perfection d'escrire ny de peindre:
Sans plus ils gastent l'encre, & broyant la couleur
Barbouillent un portrait d'inutile valeur.

L'autre preside à ceux qui ont la fantasie
Esprise ardentement du feu de Poësie,
Qui n'abusent du nom, mais à la verité
Sont remplis de frayeur & de divinité.
Quatre ou cinq seulement sont apparus au monde,
De Grecque nation, qui ont à la faconde
Accouplé le mystere, & d'un voile divers
Par fables ont caché le vray sens de leurs vers,
A fin que le vulgaire, amy de l'ignorance,
Ne comprist le mestier de leur belle science,
Vulgaire qui se mocque, & qui met à mespris
Les mysteres sacrez, quand il les a compris.
Ils furent les premiers qui la Theologie
Et le sçavoir hautain de nostre Astrologie,
Par un art tressubtil de fables ont voilé,
Et des yeux ignorans du peuple reculé.

Dieu les tient agitez, & jamais ne les laisse,
D'un aguillon ardant il les picque & les presse.
Ils ont les pieds à terre & l'esprit dans les Cieux,
Le peuple les estime enragez, furieux,
Ils errent par les bois, par les monts, par les prées,
Et jouyssent tous seuls des Nymphes & des Fées.

  Entre ces deux mestiers, un mestier s'est trouvé,
Qui, tenant le milieu, pour bon est approuvé,
Et Dieu l'a concedé aux hommes, pour les faire
Apparoistre en renom par dessus le vulgaire,
Duquel se sont polis mille autres artisans,
Lesquels sont estimez entre les mieux disans:
Par un vers heroïque ils ont mis en histoire
Des Princes & des Rois la proesse & la gloire,
Et comme serviteurs de Belone & de Mars
Ont au son de leurs vers animé les soldars.
Ils ont sur l'eschaffaut par feinctes presentée
La vie des humains en deux sortes chantée,
Imitant des grands Rois la triste affection
Et des peuples menus la commune action.
La plainte des Seigneurs fut dicte Tragedie,
L'action du commun fut dicte Comedie.
L'argument du Comicque est de toutes saisons,
Mais celuy du Tragicque est de peu de maisons:
D'Athenes, Troye, Argos, de Thebes & Mycenes
Sont pris les argumens qui conviennent aux scenes.
Rome t'en a donné, que nous voyons icy,
Et crains que les François ne t'en donnent aussi.

  Jodelle le premier, d'une plainte hardie,
Françoisement chanta la Grecque Tragedie,
Puis, en changeant de ton, chanta devant nos Rois
La jeune Comedie en langage François,
Et si bien les sonna, que Sophocle & Menandre,
Tant fussent-ils sçavans, y eussent peu apprandre:
Et toy, Grevin, apres, toy mon Grevin encor,
Qui dores ton menton d'un petit crespe d'or,

A qui vingt & deux ans n'ont pas clos les années,
Tu nous as toutesfois les Muses amenées,
Et nous as surmontez, qui sommes jà grisons,
Et qui pensions avoir Phebus en nos maisons.
  Amour premierement te blesse la poictrine
Du dart venant des yeux d'une beauté divine,
Qu'en mille beaux papiers tu as chanté[e] à fin
Qu'une si belle ardeur ne prenne jamais fin.
Puis tu voulus sçavoir des herbes la nature,
Tu te feis Medecin, & d'une ardente cure
Doublement agité, tu appris les mestiers
D'Apollon, qui t'estime et te suit volontiers,
A fin qu'en nostre France un seul GREVIN assemble
La docte Medecine & les vers tout ensemble.[1]

[1] Laum., vol. XIV, p. 193. First published at the beginning of the *Théâtre de J. Grévin* (Paris, 1561).

VIII

HYMNE DE L'AUTONNE
A
MONSIEUR DE LAUBESPINE

Le jour que je fu né, le Daimon qui preside
Aux Muses me servit en ce Monde de guide,
M'anima d'un esprit gaillard & vigoreux,
Et me fist de science & d'honneur amoureux.
   En lieu des grands thresors & de richesses veines,
Qui aveuglent les yeux des personnes humaines,
Me donna pour partage une fureur d'esprit,
Et l'art de bien coucher ma verve par escrit.
Il me haussa le cueur, haussa la fantasie,
M'inspirant dedans l'ame un don de Poësie,
Que Dieu n'a concedé qu'à l'esprit agité
Des poignans aiguillons de sa divinité.
   Quand l'homme en est touché, il devient un prophete,
Il predit toute chose avant qu'elle soit faite,
Il cognoist la nature, & les secrets des cieux,
Et d'un esprit boüillant s'esleve entre les Dieux.
Il cognoist la vertu des herbes & des pierres,
Il enferme les vents, il charme les tonnerres,
Sciences que le peuple admire, & ne scait pas
Que Dieu les va donnant aux hommes d'icy-bas,
Quand ils ont de l'humain les ames separées,
Et qu'à telle fureur elles sont preparées,
Par oraison, par jeune, & penitence aussi,
Dont aujourd'huy le monde a bien peu de souci.
   Car Dieu ne communique aux hommes ses mysteres
S'ils ne sont vertueux, devots & solitaires,

Eslongnés des tyrans, & des peuples qui ont
La malice en la main, & l'impudence au front,
Brulés d'ambition, & tourmentés d'envie,
Qui leur sert de bourreau tout le temps de leur vie.

Je n'avois pas quinze ans que les mons & les boys,
Et les eaux me plaisoient plus que la court des Roys,
Et les noires forests espesses de ramées,
Et du bec des oyseaux les roches entamées:
Une valée, un antre en horreur obscurcy,
Un desert effroiable, estoit tout mon soucy,
Afin de voir au soir les Nymphes & les Fées
Danser desoubs la Lune en cotte par les prées,
Fantastique d'esprit: & de voir les Sylvains
Estre boucs par les pieds, & hommes par les mains,
Et porter sur le front des cornes en la sorte
Q'un petit aignelet de quatre moys les porte.

J'allois apres la danse & craintif je pressois
Mes pas dedans le trac des Nymphes, & pensois,
Que pour mettre mon pied en leur trace poudreuse
J'aurois incontinent l'ame plus genereuse,
Ainsi que l'Ascrean qui gravement sonna,
Quand l'une des neuf Sœurs du laurier luy donna.

Or je ne fu trompé de ma douce entreprise,
Car la gentille Euterpe ayant ma dextre prise,
Pour m'oster le mortel par neuf fois me lava,
De l'eau d'une fontaine où peu de monde va,
Me charma par neuf fois, puis d'une bouche enflée
(Ayant de sur mon chef son haleine soufflée)
Me herissa le poil de crainte & de fureur,
Et me remplit le cœur d'ingenieuse erreur,
En me disant ainsi: Puisque tu veux nous suivre,
Heureux apres la mort nous te ferons revivre,
Par longue renommée, & ton los ennobly
Acablé du tombeau n'ira point en obly.

Tu seras du vulgaire appellé frenetique,
Insencé, furieux, farouche, fantastique,

Maussade, mal plaisant, car le peuple medit
De celuy qui de mœurs aux siennes contredit.

Mais courage, Ronsard, les plus doctes poëtes,
Les Sybilles, Devins, Augures & Prophetes,
Huiez, siflez, moquez des peuples ont esté:
Et toutesfois, Ronsard, ils disoient verité.

N'espere d'amasser de grands biens en ce Monde,
Une forest, un pré, une montaigne, une onde
Sera ton heritage, & seras plus heureux
Que ceux qui vont cachant tant de thresors chez eux:
Tu n'auras point de peur qu'un Roy de sa tempeste
Te vienne en moins d'un jour écarboüiller la teste,
Ou confisquer tes biens: mais tout paisible & coy,
Tu vivras dans les boys pour la Muse & pour toy.

Ainsi disoit la Nymphe, & de là je vins estre
Disciple de d'Aurat, qui long temps fut mon maistre,
M'aprist la Poësie, & me montra comment
On doit feindre & cacher les fables proprement,
Et à bien deguiser la verité des choses
D'un fabuleux manteau dont elles sont encloses:
J'apris en sa maison à immortalizer
Les hommes que je veux celebrer & priser,
Leur donnant de mes biens, ainsi que je te donne
Pour present immortel l'hymne de cet Autonne...[1]

[1] Laum., vol. XII, p. 46 (first 86 lines only). First published in the first
of the *Trois livres du Recueil des nouvelles poesies* (Paris, 1564).

IX

LA SALADE

A AMA. JAMYN

Lave ta main blanche, gaillarde & nette,
Suy mes talons, aporte une serviette,
Allon cueillir la salade, & faison
Part à noz ans des fruitz de la saison.
D'un vague pas, d'une veuë escartée,
Deçà delà jettée & rejettée,
Or' sur la rive, ores sur un fossé,
Or' sur un champ en paresse laissé
Du laboureur, qui de luy-mesme aporte
Sans cultiver herbes de toute sorte,
Je m'en iray solitaire à l'escart.

    Tu t'en iras, Jamyn, d'une autre part
Chercher songneux, la boursette toffüe,
La pasquerette à la fueille menuë,
La pimprenelle heureuse pour le sang,
Et pour la ratte, & pour le mal de flanc,
Et je cueill'ray, compagne de la mousse,
La responsette à la racine douce,
Et le bouton de nouveaux groiseliers
Qui le Printemps annoncent les premiers.

    Puis en lysant l'ingenieux Ovide
En ces beaux vers où d'Amour il est guide,
Regangnerons le logis pas à pas:
Là recoursant jusqu'au coude nos bras,
Nous laverons nos herbes à main pleine
Au cours sacré de ma belle fonteine,

La blanchirons de sel en meinte part,
L'arrouserons de vinaigre rosart,
L'engresserons de l'huille de Provence:
L'huille qui vient aux oliviers de France
Rompt l'estomac, & ne vaut du tout rien.

Voilà, Jamyn, voilà mon souv'rain bien,
En attendant que de mes veines parte
Cette execrable horrible fiebvre quarte
Qui me consomme & le corps & le cœur
Et me fait vivre en extreme langueur.

Tu me diras que la fiebvre m'abuze,
Que je suis fol, ma salade & ma Muse:
Tu diras vray: je le veux estre aussy,
Telle fureur me guarist mon soucy.
Tu me diras que la vie est meilleure
Des importuns, qui vivent à toute heure
Aupres des Grandz en credit, & bonheur,
Enorgueilliz de pompes & d'honneur:
Je le sçay bien, mais je ne le veuz faire,
Car telle vie à la mienne est contraire.

Il faut mentir, flater, & courtizer,
Rire sans ris, sa face deguiser
Au front d'autruy, & je ne le veux faire,
Car telle vie à la mienne est contraire.
Je suis pour suivre à la trace une Court,
Trop maladif, trop paresseux, & sourd,
Et trop creintif: au reste je demande
Un doux repos, & ne veux plus qu'on pende
Comme un pongnard, les soucis sur mon front.

En peu de temps les Courtizans s'en vont
En chef grison, ou meurent sur un coffre.
Dieu pour salaire un tel present leur offre
D'avoir gasté leur gentil naturel
D'ambition & de bien temporel,
Un bien mondain, qui s'enfuit à la trace,
Dont ne jouïst l'acquereur, ny sa race:

Ou bien, Jamin, ilz n'auront point d'enfans,
Ou ilz seront en la fleur de leurs ans
Disgratiez par Fortune ou par vice,
Ou ceux qu'ilz ont retrompez d'artifice
Les apastant par subtilles raisons,
Feront au Ciel voller leurs oraisons:
    Dieu s'en courrouce, & veux qu'un pot de terre
Soit foudroyé, sans qu'il face la guerre
Contre le Ciel, & serve qu'en tout lieu
L'Ambition est desplaisante à Dieu,
Et la faveur qui n'est que vaine bouë,
Dont le destin en nous moquant se jouë:
D'où la Fortune aux retours inconstans
A la parfin les tombe malcontens,
Montrant à tous par leur cheute soudaine
Que c'est du vent que la farce mondaine,
Et que l'home est tresmal'heureux qui vit
En court estrange, & meurt loing de son lit.
    Loing de moy soit la faveur & la pompe,
Qui d'aparence, en se fardant, nous trompe,
Ains qui nous lime & nous ronge au dedans
D'ambition & de soucis mordans.
L'ambition, les soucis & l'envie,
Et tout cela qui meurdrist nostre vie,
Semblent des Dieux à tels hommes, qui n'ont
Ny foy au cœur, ny honte sur le front:
Telz hommes sont colosses inutilles,
Beaux par dehors, dedans pleins de chevilles,
Barres & clous qui serrent ces grandz corps:
En les voyant dorez par le dehors,
Un Jupiter, Appollon, ou Neptune,
Chacun revere & doute leur fortune:
Et toutefois tel ouvrage trompeur,
Par sa haulteur ne fait seulement peur
Qu'aux idiotz: mais l'home qui est sage
Passant par là ne fait cas de l'ouvrage:

Ains en esprit il desdaigne ces Dieux,
Portraits de plastre, & luy fachent les yeux,
Subjets aux vents, au froid & à la poudre.
Le pauvre sot qui voit rougir la foudre
A longs rayons dedans leur dextre main,
Ou le trident à trois pointes d'airain,
Craint & pallist devant si grand Colosse,
Qui n'a vertu que l'aparence grosse,
Lourde, pesante, & qui ne peut en rien
Aux regardans faire ny mal ny bien,
Sinon aux fatz, où la sottize abonde,
Qui à credit craignent le rien du Monde.

    Les pauvres sotz dignes de tous mechefz
Ne sçavent pas que c'est un jeu d'eschetz
Que nostre courte & miserable vie,
E qu'aussy tost que la Mort l'a ravie
Dedans le sac somes mis à la fois
Tous pesle mesle, & Laboureurs & Rois,
Valetz, Seigneurs en mesme sepulture.
Telle est la loy de la bonne Nature,
Et de la Terre, en son ventre qui prend
De fosse egalle & le Pauvre & le Grand,
Et montre bien que la gloire mondaine,
Et la grandeur est une chose vaine.

    Ah! que me plaist ce vers Virgilian
Où le vieillard pere Corytian
Avecq' sa marre en travaillant cultive
A tour de bras sa terre non oysive
Et vers le soir sans achepter si cher
Vin en taverne, ou chair chez le boucher,
Alloit chargeant sa table de viandes,
Qui luy sembloient plus douces & friandes
Avec la faim, que celles des Seigneurs
Pleines de pompe & de fardez honneurs,
Qui, desdaigneux, de cent viandes changent
Sans aucun goust: car sans goust ilz les mangent.

Lequel des deux estoit le plus heureux,
Ou ce grand Crasse en escus plantureux,
Qui pour n'avoir les honneurs de Pompée
Alla sentir la Parthienne espée,
Ou ce vieillard qui son champ cultivoit
Et sans voir Rome en son jardin vivoit?

   Si nous sçavions, ce disoit Hesiode,
Combien nous sert l'asphodelle, & la mode
De l'acoutrer, heureux l'home seroit,
Et la Moitié le Tout surpasseroit:
Par la Moitié il entendoit la vie
Sans aucun fard des laboureurs suivie,
Qui vivent sains du labeur de leurs doigtz,
Et par le Tout les delices des Rois.
La Nature est, ce dit le bon Horace,
De peu contente, & nostre humaine race
Ne quiert beaucoup: mais nous la corrompons
Et par le trop Nature nous trompons.

   C'est trop presché: donne moy ma salade:
El' ne vaut rien (dis-tu) pour un malade!

   Hé! quoy, Jamyn, tu fais le Medecin!
Laisse moy vivre au moins jusqu'à la fin
Tout à mon aise, & ne sois triste Augure
Soit à ma vie ou à ma mort future,
Car tu ne peux, ny moy, pour tout secours
Faire plus longs ou plus petis mes jours:
Il faut charger la barque Stygieuse:
«La barque, c'est la Biere sommeilleuse,
«Faite en bateau: le naistre est le trepas:
«Sans naistre icy l'home ne mourroit pas:
«Fol qui d'ailleurs autre bien se propose,
«Naissance & mort est une mesme chose.[1]

[1] Laum., vol. XV, p. 76. First published in the *Sixiesme livre des Poemes* (Paris, 1569).

X

SONET

Je vous donne des œufs. L'œuf en sa forme ronde
Semble au Ciel, qui peut tout en ses bras enfermer,
Le feu, l'air et la terre, et l'humeur de la mer,
Et sans estre comprins comprend tout en ce monde.

La taye semble à l'air, et la glere feconde
Semble à la mer qui fait toutes choses germer;
L'aubin ressemble au feu qui peut tout animer,
La coque en pesanteur comme la terre abonde.

Et le Ciel et les œufs de blancheur sont couvers.
Je vous donne, en donnant un œuf, tout l'Univers:
Divin est le present, s'il vous est agreable.

Mais bien qu'il soit parfait, il ne peut egaler
Vostre perfection qui n'a point de semblable,
Dont les Dieux seulement sont dignes de parler.[1]

[1] Cohen, vol. I, p. 324. First published among the *Amours diverses* in the collected edition *Œuvres* (Paris, 1578).

XI

ELEGIE

Quiconque aura premier la main embesongnée
A te couper, forest, d'une dure congnée,
Qu'il puisse s'enferrer de son propre baston,
Et sente en l'estomac la faim d'Erisichthon,
Qui coupa de Cerés le chesne venerable,
Et qui, gourmand de tout, de tout insatiable,
Les bœufs et les moutons de sa mere esgorgea,
Puis, pressé de la faim, soy-mesme se mangea.
Ainsi puisse engloutir ses rentes et sa terre,
Et se devore apres par les dents de la guerre.
Qu'il puisse pour vanger le sang de nos forests,
Tousjours nouveaux emprunts sur nouveaux interests
Devoir à l'usurier, et qu'en fin il consomme
Tout son bien à payer la principale somme.
Que, tousjours sans repos, ne face en son cerveau
Que tramer pour-neant quelque dessein nouveau,
Porté d'impatience et de fureur diverse,
Et de mauvais conseil qui les hommes renverse.
Escoute, bucheron, arreste un peu le bras,
Ce ne sont pas des bois que tu jettes à bas,
Ne vois-tu pas le sang, lequel degoute à force
Des Nymphes qui vivoyent dessous la dure escorce?
Sacrilege meurdrier, si on pend un voleur
Pour piller un butin de bien peu de valeur,
Combien de feux, de fers, de morts, et de destresses
Merites-tu, meschant, pour tuer des Deesses?
Forest, haute maison des oiseaux bocagers,
Plus le cerf solitaire et les chevreuls legers

Ne paistront sous ton ombre, et ta verte criniere
Plus du soleil d'esté ne rompra la lumiere.
Plus l'amoureux pasteur, sur un tronq adossé,
Enflant son flageolet à quatre trous persé,
Son mastin à ses pieds, à son flanc la houlette,
Ne dira plus l'ardeur de sa belle Janette;
Tout deviendra muet, Echo sera sans voix,
Tu deviendras campagne, et, en lieu de tes bois,
Dont l'ombrage incertain lentement se remue,
Tu sentiras le soc, le coutre et la charrue.
Tu perdras ton silence, et, haletans d'effroy,
Ny Satyres, ny Pans ne viendront plus chez toy.
Adieu, vieille forest, le jouët de Zephyre,
Où premier j'accorday les langues de ma lyre,
Où premier j'entendi les fleches resonner
D'Apollon, qui me vint tout le cœur estonner;
Où premier admirant la belle Calliope,
Je devins amoureux de sa neuvaine trope,
Quand sa main sur le front cent roses me jetta,
Et de son propre laict Euterpe m'allaita.
Adieu, vieille forest, adieu, testes sacrées,
De tableaux et de fleurs autrefois honorées,
Maintenant le desdain des passans alterez,
Qui bruslez en esté des rayons etherez,
Sans plus trouver le frais de tes douces verdures,
Accusent vos meurtriers, et leur disent injures.
Adieu, chesnes, couronne aux vaillans citoyens,
Arbres de Jupiter, germes Dodonéens,
Qui premiers aux humains donnastes à repaistre,
Peuples vrayment ingrats, qui n'ont sceu recognoistre
Les biens receus de vous, peuples vraiment grossiers,
De massacrer ainsi nos peres nourriciers.
Que l'homme est malheureux qui au monde se fie!
O Dieux, que veritable est la philosophie,
Qui dit que toute chose à la fin perira,
Et qu'en changeant de forme une autre vestira.

De Tempé la vallée un jour sera montagne,
Et la cyme d'Athos une large campagne,
Neptune quelquefois de blé sera couvert:
La matiere demeure, et la forme se perd.[1]

[1] Cohen, vol. II, p. 116. First published in the *Œuvres* (Paris, 1584).

XII

ELEGIE

Six ans estoient coulez, et la septiesme annee
Estoit presques entiere en ses pas retournee,
Quand loin d'affection, de desir et d'amour,
En pure liberté je passois tout le jour,
Et franc de tout soucy qui les ames devore,
Je dormois dés le soir jusqu'au point de l'aurore.
Car seul maistre de moy j'allois plein de loisir,
Où le pied me portoit, conduit de mon desir,
Ayant tousjours és mains pour me servir de guide
Aristote ou Platon, ou le docte Euripide,
Mes bons hostes muets, qui ne faschent jamais:
Ainsi que je les prens, ainsi je les remais.
O douce compagnie et utile et honneste!
Un autre en caquetant m'estourdiroit la teste.
Puis du livre ennuyé, je regardois les fleurs,
Fueilles, tiges, rameaux, especes et couleurs,
Et l'entrecoupement de leurs formes diverses,
Peintes de cent façons, jaunes, rouges et perses,
Ne me pouvant saouler, ainsi qu'en un tableau,
D'admirer la Nature, et ce qu'elle a de beau,
Et de dire en parlant aux fleurettes escloses,
Celuy est presque Dieu qui cognoist toutes choses,
Esloigné du vulgaire, et loin des courtizans,
De fraude et de malice impudens artizans.
Tantost j'errois seulet par les forests sauvages
Sur les bords enjonchez des peinturez rivages,
Tantost par les rochers reculez et deserts,
Tantost par les taillis, verte maison des cerfs.

J'aimois le cours suivy d'une longue riviere,
Et voir onde sur onde allonger sa carriere,
Et flot à l'autre flot en roulant s'attacher,
Et pendu sur le bord me plaisoit d'y pescher,
Estant plus resjouy d'une chasse muette
Troubler des escaillez la demeure secrette,
Tirer avecq' la ligne en tremblant emporté
Le credule poisson prins à l'haim apasté,
Qu'un grand Prince n'est aise ayant prins à la chasse
Un cerf qu'en haletant tout un jour il pourchasse.
Heureux, si vous eussiez d'un mutuel esmoy
Prins l'apast amoureux aussi bien comme moy,
Que tout seul j'avallay, quand par trop desireuse
Mon ame en vos yeux beut le poison amoureuse.
Puis alors que Vesper vient embrunir nos yeux,
Attaché dans le ciel je contemple les cieux,
En qui Dieu nous escrit en notes non obscures
Les sorts et les destins de toutes creatures.
Car luy, en desdaignant, comme font les humains,
D'avoir encre et papier et plume entre les mains,
Par les astres du ciel qui sont ses characteres,
Les choses nous predit et bonnes et contraires.
Mais les hommes chargez de terre et du trespas
Mesprisent tel escrit, et ne le lisent pas.
Or le plus de mon bien pour decevoir ma peine,
C'est de boire à longs traits les eaux de la fontaine
Qui de vostre beau nom se brave, et en courant
Par les prez vos honneurs va tousjours murmurant,
Et la Royne se dit des eaux de la contree,
Tant vault le gentil soin d'une Muse sacree,
Qui peult vaincre la mort, et les sorts inconstans,
Sinon pour tout jamais, au moins pour un long temps.
Là, couché dessus l'herbe, en mes discours je pense
Que pour aimer beaucoup j'ay peu de recompense,
Et que mettre son cœur aux Dames si avant,
C'est vouloir peindre en l'onde, et arrester le vent,

M'asseurant toutefois qu'alors que le vieil âge
Aura comme un sorcier changé vostre visage,
Et lors que vos cheveux deviendront argentez,
Et que vos yeux, d'amour ne seront plus hantez,
Que tousjours vous aurez, si quelque soin vous touche,
En l'esprit mes escrits, mon nom en vostre bouche.
Maintenant que voicy l'an septiéme venir,
Ne pensez plus Helene en vos laqs me tenir.
La raison m'en delivre, et vostre rigueur dure,
Puis il fault que mon age obeysse à Nature.[1]

[1] Cohen, vol. I, p. 276. First published among the *Œuvres* (Paris, 1584).

Index